SURFMAN
The Adventures of a Coast Guard Dog

By Colonel S. P. MEEK

ALFRED · A · KNOPF : *New York*

1950

THIS IS A BORZOI BOOK,
PUBLISHED BY ALFRED A. KNOPF, INC.

COPYRIGHT 1950 BY S. P. MEEK AND EDNA NOBLE MEEK. All rights reserved. No part of this book may be reproduced in any form without permission in writing from the publisher, except by a reviewer who may quote brief passages and reproduce not more than three illustrations in a review to be printed in a magazine or newspaper. Manufactured in the United States of America. Published simultaneously in Canada by McClelland & Steward Limited.

FIRST EDITION

To

ALICE and BOB NOBLE

Preface

THIS IS ANOTHER OF THOSE BOOKS that have been many years in the planning and writing. I first conceived the idea almost twenty years ago when I was stationed in Hawaii. Among my friends there I numbered Commander (now Commodore, U.S.C.G., Retired) Jack Baylis, skipper of the Coast Guard Cutter *Itasca*. It was while I was having lunch with him in the *Itasca*'s wardroom that he asked me why I didn't write a book with a Coast Guard background.

At that time most of my books had an army background and the idea of a change sounded good, although I realized it would involve a great deal of research before I could learn enough about the Coast Guard to make such a book even reasonably authentic. But the idea did appeal to me and five years later, when I was stationed in San Francisco, I visited the Coast Guard District Office with the idea of starting to gather material. I was given the proper clearance and visited several installations in and near San Francisco, but that was as far as I could get at that time. I did not have the time, nor could I do the extensive travel which I soon saw would be necessary. The idea fizzled out and the only result was a single scene in *Rusty*, the book on which I was then working.

The idea lay fallow for a number of years until my retirement from active service gave me both the time and the opportunity to travel. On one of my trips to New York I had occasion to discuss plans for future books with my publishers. One of their first suggestions was for a book with a Coast Guard background. I laughed and took from my pocket a letter from Captain S. F. Gray, Chief of the Public Information Division of the Coast Guard, making an appointment with me for lunch in Washington a few days later.

Captain Gray and I spent the best part of a day together and when I left Washington my plans were quite definite. I would finish *Hans*, which I was going to Florida to prepare, then I would report to the Commandant of the 7th Coast Guard District at Miami with a clearance from Captain Gray and there prepare a schedule for visits to 7th District installations. I carried out this plan and was passed along from one Coast Guard district to the next. During the spring and summer I visited selected installations along the Atlantic coast from Loggerhead Key in Florida to Cape Ann in Massachusetts.

Preface

I soon found that I could not hope to cover all, or even a major part, of the multitudinous duties devolving on the personnel of the Coast Guard. Everything was open to me, I could go where I pleased and see anything I wished, but there were too many places to go and too much to see. If I tried to cover the work of the cutters; the ice patrol, the weather patrol, the Bering Sea patrol, the Alaskan patrol, to name only a few; it would take me years, not months, to gather my material. Even had I done so, I would still leave uncovered the work of the vitally important Search and Rescue, the Aids to Navigation Division and a dozen more types of Coast Guard work.

I did try. I made a short cruise, I flew with Search and Rescue planes, I watched navigation aids being replaced, serviced and repaired, I visited lighthouses, but the phase of their work which appealed most strongly to me was the Lifesaving Service, the Life Boat Stations, and it was on this work that I soon began to concentrate. Perhaps the royal welcome I received from them had something to do with my decision. Many of the Life Boat Stations are in very isolated spots and a visitor was a welcome novelty. If nothing more, he was fresh blood for the checker tournaments and the horseshoe pitching games.

They waived formality and took me in as one of

themselves. I lived at the stations, ate at the messes, stood tower watch with them and rode with them on rescue calls. I saw surfboats launched and beach apparatus drills. I rode in jeeps, command cars and ducks. I went clamming and fishing with them. I even helped to dig out a stopped up septic tank. It was lots of fun and I met with a friendliness and hospitality that could not be surpassed. The only difficulty I met with was in getting them to tell me of their exploits. They never felt they had done anything out of the ordinary. They had a job to do. They did it. So what was the use of talking about it afterwards?

A typical example of this met me at Chicamacomico. I pointed out to Levene Midgett, the commanding officer, a wreck on the beach near the station and asked about it. It looked rather recent.

"Oh, that?" Levene said. "Oh, she came ashore at night, a year ago last February. We went down and tossed them a line and hauled them ashore."

That was it. Period. No story. It took me hours of patient digging to learn that the rescue was made in the darkness with a ninety-mile gale blowing, that the first two shots from the Lyle gun went wild due to the wind, that the sand anchor pulled out and the hawser had to be anchored to a command car, and finally that one of the rescued men froze to the hawser and one of the station crew had to go out along the swaying rope, hand over hand, to break his hold and return him to the breeches buoy to be hauled ashore. But there was no story in that. They just had a job to do and they went out and did it. Why talk about it later? They were much more interested in discussing the possibility of the highway being extended from Avon to Rodanthe.

While I covered most of the Atlantic coast in my travels, I found most of my material in three areas: Cape Cod, Long Island and the Outer Banks of North Carolina. The last of these I chose for my locale, both for its picturesqueness and for the fact that there, above everywhere else, the Coast Guard is a vital part of the daily lives of the inhabitants. Four out of five Outer Banks families have one or more members in the Coast Guard and I met men who were the fifth and sixth generation of their families in the Lifesaving Service. The names of Midgett, Meekins, Gray, Scarborough, Barrett, Austin, Piggot, Burras, O'Neal and a dozen more loom large in the annals of the Coast Guard. At one station I visited, out of a roster of 11 men, there were 4 Midgetts, 2 Meekinses, 2 Scarboroughs, 1 Burras and 1 Austin, and none of them claimed to be related to one another!

Once my locale was decided upon, the choice of my hero became automatic. The most popular breed of dogs along the Outer Banks (and at Life Boat

Stations in general, for that matter) is the Chesapeake retriever, or the Chesapeake Bay dog, as he is also frequently called. The Chesapeake is probably the finest performer in the water of any breed. They are tremendously powerful swimmers and no surf will daunt them or make their courage fail.

Surfman, however, is not the story of any one dog. He is built up from the characters and credited with the exploits of a number of dogs of the same breed whom I met or of whom I was told at the various stations I visited. They were wonderful dogs with a great record for the actual saving of lives.

The Chesapeake is not a demonstrative breed nor overly affectionate, except to their masters, but they are usually polite, even if a bit reserved, to strangers. Still, their friendship can be won and I flatter myself that I left some good canine friends behind when I departed from the Outer Banks. And if Fondy, Maggie Jones, Barnacle Bill, Rajah, or any of my other Chesapeake friends feel that I have done them an injustice by appropriating their actual exploits and crediting them to the mythical Surfman, I offer to each my humble apologies.

S. P. Meek,
COLONEL, U.S. ARMY, RETIRED

Nags Head, North Carolina

Acknowledgments

I WOULD LIKE TO EXPRESS my appreciation to all of the Coast Guard personnel with whom I came in contact along the Atlantic coast for their uniform courtesy, helpfulness and hospitality. My thanks are especially due to the following:

    Captain S. F. Gray, *Public Information Division, Office of the Commandant*

    Captain P. B. Cronk, *Chief of Operations, 1st Coast Guard District*

    Captain I. E. Eskridge, *Chief of Staff, 5th Coast Guard District*

    Commander G. P. McGowan, *Public Relations Officer, 5th Coast Guard District*

    Lieutenant Commander T. E. Midgett, *U.S.C.G., Retired, Kitty Hawk, N. C.*

    Lieutenant Frank Rados, *U.S.C.G. Cutter Mariposa*

    Lieutenant J. A. Heikel, *Moriches Life Boat Station*

    Lieutenant (j.g.) W. E. Ireland, *Cape Cod Canal Life Boat Station*

Lieutenant (j.g.) H. W. Rollinson, *U.S.C.G. Cutter Arbutus*
Lieutenant (j.g.) M. H. Twiford, *Eaton's Neck Life Boat Station*
Lieutenant (j.g.) D. H. Miner, *Ponce de Leon Life Boat Station*
Chief Boatswain Alfred Volton, *Race Point Life Boat Station*
Chief Boatswain George Harrison Meekins, *Oregon Inlet Life Boat Station*
Chief Boatswain Julian L. Gray, *Fort Pierce Inlet Life Boat Station*
Boatswain E. M. Pike, *Ditch Plains Life Boat Station*
Chief Boatswain's Mate Pennel A. Tillet, *Cape Hatteras Life Boat Station*
Chief Boatswain's Mate Levene W. Midgett, *Chicamacomico Life Boat Station*
Chief Boatswain's Mate Nevin W. Westcott, *Nags Head Life Boat Station*
Chief Machinist's Mate Warren Bennett, *Hillsboro Inlet Light*
Boatswain's Mate (first class) A. W. Jones, *Montauk Point Light*
Journalist (first class) Alex Haley, *3rd Coast Guard District*
Mr. D. V. Meekins, Editor, *The Coastland Times, Manteo, N. C.*
Mr. Ben D. McNeill, *Buxton, N. C.*

Contents

Prologue	3
THE OUTER BANKS	14
JEFF DAVIS MACALPIN	34
A MATTER OF HISTORY	46
ROUTINE CALL	57
OLD JOEY	78
TOWER WATCH	94
THE DUCK GOES OUT	104
THE *Damficare*	124
SURFMAN REDEEMS HIMSELF	138
MISSING	159
THE SEARCH	170
JOEY TRIES TO REMEMBER	182
HURRICANE	198
"DISTRESS ROCKETS AT SEA, SIR!"	209

Contents xviii

RESCUE 219

A MATTER OF JUSTICE 242

Appendix:

    I. THE UNITED STATES COAST GUARD 251
   II. THE CAPE HATTERAS LIGHT 260
  III. THE PHONETIC ALPHABET 264
  IV. BEAUFORT'S SCALE 266

SURFMAN

The Adventures of a Coast Guard Dog

Prologue

THE WIND, which had been blowing with gale force for hours, rose to a shrieking crescendo. The Cape Hatteras Life Boat Station trembled before its onslaught and the lanterns in the recreation room flickered in the drafts which forced their way through the window casings, despite the storm shutters which had been bolted tightly in place early in the day.

Two surfmen looked up from the checker board which had engrossed their attention ever since the evening meal and listened with critical ears to the howl of the wind.

"Sixty-five," one of them remarked. "Maybe seventy."

"Eighty or better," the other retorted.

The first speaker snorted in disgust.

"Why not a hundred and fifty?" he asked sarcastically. "It doesn't cost any more."

"Because it's not blowing a hundred and fifty. It's somewhere between eighty and ninety."

"I'll kiss your foot twice for every mile over seventy-five. How about it, Chief?"

Tommy Holmes looked up from his magazine.

"Go look at the anemometer,"* he said mildly. "All I know is that I'm glad I'm here and not out on the Diamond Shoals lightship."

There was a grunt of assent from the surfmen. Several of them had served on a lightship in the past and realized the truth of the Chief's words. They were in a comfortable place and, so long as a ship did not get into trouble off shore, they could stay there, except for the three unfortunates who were on the north and south beach patrols and on the tower watch. If a ship did get into trouble—Well, that was what they were there for and the motto of the Coast Guard was *Semper Paratus*, Always Ready.

The checker players returned to their game. Neither of them was certain enough about his estimate of the wind velocity to be anxious to put it to the test and neither of them cared to climb the lookout tower in the teeth of the gale until it was time to relieve the watcher on duty. That time would come soon enough, for each man took his turn in the round-the-clock watch over the beach and sea that

---

*an instrument which measures the velocity of the wind

was maintained from the tower's vantage point.

The chronometer struck five bells. Holmes yawned, stretched, then put down his magazine and rose slowly.

"I think I'll turn in," he said in his mild voice. "Tomorrow will be another day."

He started slowly in the direction of his quarters. With a crash, the door of the recreation room burst open and the resulting gust of wind swept the papers and magazines from the table. Framed in the doorway was the tower watch.

"Distress rockets at sea, Chief!" he reported.

Every trace of lethargy and mildness vanished from Holmes' bearing. In an instant he was taut and ready, his face stern and alert.

"Where away?" he demanded.

"About three miles north and maybe two miles off the beach."

Holmes' orders came with machine gun rapidity.

"Turn to, all hands! Boots and oilskins. Kennedy, start the tractor and hook to the pulling boat. Dewey, call Little Kinnakeet and ask them to join us with their beach apparatus; we can't take ours and the boat too. Then call Chicamacomico and tell them to stand by. Where's Stanton Truslow?"

"On the south beach patrol, Chief."

"Burn a Coston light to recall him, I'll need him at stroke oar."

The surfmen cast quick glances at one another, then looked at the Chief. Surely no one in his right senses would think of trying to launch a surfboat in the teeth of the offshore gale that was blowing. Even if they could get it water-borne, the surf would pick it up and toss it back onto the beach. Holmes' face grew even more stern and forbidding as they faced him.

"*Turn to!*" His voice cracked like a whiplash. "Wrecks don't usually hold together more than a week, you know."

There was a thudding of feet as the surfmen ran for the locker room. Five minutes later they were trotting along beside the surfboat, steadying it with outstretched hands as the boat wagon on which it rested wobbled and swayed along over the rough sand in the wake of Kennedy's tractor. Far ahead of them, on the water's edge, they could see the red glow of a Coston light burned by the north beach patrol, both to guide them to the scene and to inform the doomed ship that their distress signals had been seen and that help was on the way. Behind them a similar light glowed from the lookout tower to call the missing Stanton Truslow back from the south patrol to his post of duty at the stroke oar of the surfboat.

It was almost an hour before Kennedy turned the tractor toward the pounding surf and dragged the boat wagon over the ridge that separated them from the beach. As they unlatched the surfboat from the cradle and lowered it to the sand, the crew from Little Kinnakeet Life Boat Station trotted up, dragging their beach cart with its Lyle gun behind them.

"We can't use the gun, Davy," Holmes told the Chief of the Little Kinnakeet Station. "She's fast on the inner reef, a good mile and a half off shore. I'll have to take the boat out. Let me have your best oarsman; I'm one short of a crew."

A Little Kinnakeet man joined the Cape Hatteras crew and, under Holmes' direction, they slid the surfboat along the sand until it was at the edge of the pounding surf. Life preservers were taken from the boat and each oarsman donned one.

"Scarsdale bow, Truslow stroke," Holmes' voice rang out, audible even over the roar of the wind and the crash of the surf. "Double-bank center oars. Where's Truslow?" he shouted as no one took the station of the stroke oarsman. "TRUSLOW!"

"Not here yet, Chief," one of the men reported.

Holmes hesitated. Without the husky Truslow who always rowed the stroke oar, the problem of launching the boat became more complicated. The Chief of the Little Kinnakeet Station made his way forward.

"You're not going to try to launch in this surf, are you, Tommy?" he asked.

"Of course I'm launching. Regulations say we have to go out, don't they?"

"You may get out, but you'll never get back."

"Regulations don't say we have to get back, Davy, just that we have to go out. But I'll miss my stroke oar."

"I'll stroke for you, Tommy. I'm not Truslow, but I'm the best here, I think."

"All right, Davy, thanks."

Chief Davidson jumped into position on the weather side of the surfboat. Holmes' eyes swept along the line to make sure all was in readiness, then he dropped to his knees.

"Into Thy hands, Oh Lord, we deliver ourselves. Do with us as seems best to Thy wisdom and Thy mercy, but we pray that none may die because we fail or falter. Grant us, if it be Thy will, an honorable end, striving in Thy service. Amen."

He rose to his feet and his voice rang out like a bugle.

"TAKE OARS!"

The oarsmen took the stout ash oars from the boat and dropped them on the thwarts, the outer ends through the thole pins. They grasped the sides of the boat and gently eased it down into the boiling water until the surf was up around the waist of the bow oarsman. Here they held it while Holmes studied the waves. The surf was running in a seven wave cycle* and he bided his time, waiting for the moment that he knew must eventually come. One complete cycle of waves rolled up on the beach, then a second and a third, but Holmes made no move. The fourth cycle started, running with even greater fury than the preceding ones. When the seventh wave broke, Scarsdale was momentarily swept from his feet, but he maintained his grip on the boat and struggled to get his feet again on the sand. For a moment the sea was comparatively calm and Holmes' voice rang through the lull.

"IN BOW!"

Scarsdale scrambled into the boat and grasped his oar. He swung it out and caught water in a valiant stroke.

"GO!"

With a mighty effort the crew ran the boat forward into the momentarily slack water. Each man, as the water swirled so high about him that he could no longer keep his feet on the sand, jumped into the boat, grasped his oar and took up the stroke which Scarsdale had already set. The rowing was a little

---

* The waves were coming in in groups of seven, each wave higher than the preceding one. When the seventh, the maximum, wave passed, there was a slight lull before the next cycle of seven began. This lull is the only time when a surfboat can be successfully launched in a heavy surf.

ragged until Davidson was in his place, then all took their stroke from him and it evened out. An instant later Holmes came in over the stern and put out the steering oar, bending his full strength against it just in time to keep the boat from broaching to as the first wave of the next cycle struck it.

As the boat straightened out on her course, Holmes' voice rang out, setting the time for the oarsmen.

"Give wa-a-a-y *together!* Give wa-a-a-y *together!* Give wa-a-a-y *together!*"

The second wave of the cycle broke about them and then the third. The boat tossed and threatened to broach, but Holmes' strength and skill on the steering oar held it on its course. Suddenly, as the fourth wave approached, his voice took on a new note of urgency and the tempo of his shouts changed.

"*Give* WAY *together! Give* WAY *together! Give* WAY *together!*"

Faster and faster the beat became until it seemed impossible that men could swing the heavy oars as rapidly as he demanded. The fourth, fifth and sixth waves broke and then came the crucial moment. The huge seventh wave rolled toward them, mountain high, and broke at their bow. The boat was lifted, tossed high, and for a moment the oars thrashed uselessly in the air. The boat dropped sickeningly and a capsize seemed to be inevitable, but Holmes bent his strength to the steering oar and held it true. Again his voice rang out, this time with a note of triumphant confidence.

"Give wa-a-a-y *together!* Give wa-a-a-y *together!* Give wa-a-a-y *together!*"

The oarsmen caught the new stroke and in the momentary lull which followed the seventh wave the boat surged forward under their efforts. The next cycle of waves came, higher and more vicious than the preceding one, but the worst of the danger was past. The boat was out beyond the point where the surf broke and while it was tossed about like a chip by the raging water, there was now little danger that it would pitch-pole* or capsize. Holmes held an iron grip on the steering oar and guided the craft over the tossing sea toward the spot where rockets were still rising from the stranded vessel.

The group of Little Kinnakeet men left on the shore, who had watched the struggle by the glare of the tractor headlights, shook hands and pounded one another on the back.

"They did it, they did it!" they exclaimed over and over again.

"Yes, sir, they did it, and with Chief Davy at stroke," one cried exultantly.

"Yeah, but I reckon Mr. Holmes would rather

---
* be thrown end over end

have had Stanton Truslow there," one of the older men replied.

"That he would," a second answered. "I wonder where Stan is?"

"Doug Scarsdale told me he was on beach patrol. They burned a light to recall him, but he didn't get here in time. He's probably slogging along up the beach now and he'll be mad as a wet hen that they went out without him."

"I should think he'd have got here unless he was clear down to Hatteras village. Mr. Holmes waited long enough before launching."

"Maybe he wasn't too anxious to get here in time," one man suggested. "I wouldn't have been if I'd been in his shoes."

"If that's the way you feel, you'd better ask for your discharge," a grizzled veteran exclaimed in a disgusted voice. "Stanton will be here in a few minutes. He's a real Coast Guardsman, like his father and grandfather were."

The veteran's prophecy proved to be a false one. Surfman Stanton Truslow did not arrive that night, nor was he ever seen again. For two months the Coast Guard waited and made an elaborate investigation, but it was fruitless. Truslow had simply disappeared without trace. On May 25, 1929, his name was dropped from the rolls of the United

States Coast Guard. The official notation after his name on the muster rolls of the Cape Hatteras Life Boat Station read, "Deserted the service in the face of danger."

The Outer Banks

"Sit down, Surfman, you make me nervous."

The big, mahogany-colored Chesapeake retriever looked up reproachfully at his master. With a myriad of new smells waiting to be investigated, carefully catalogued and then stored away in his canine memory, the command simply did not make sense to the dog. He waved his tail placatingly, then made a tentative step toward a nearby telephone pole.

"Sit down, I told you."

Morgan Graham's quiet voice was low-pitched and pleasant, but it carried a note of authority that allowed no second interpretation of his words. Surfman resigned himself to obedience and sat at his master's feet, but his twitching nose constantly tested the light breeze and his brown eyes roved the streets of Manteo.

The purr of a motor was heard in the distance and a big, ungainly looking bus, built on a Ford truck

The Outer Banks

chassis, rounded the corner and stopped in front of the terminal. The driver, a slender, light-framed young man, jumped down and helped the three passengers to unload their scanty luggage. He shoved his peaked cap onto the back of his head and grinned engagingly at Graham.

"Going my way?" he asked.

"Yes, if this is the Hatteras-Manteo bus line."

"That's what's painted on the side of it, but what the cash customers call it depends on how often it gets stuck in the sand," the driver chuckled. "Glad to have you with us. I'm Jamieson Migert, generally known as 'Junior'."

He thrust out his hand which Graham took in a firm grip.

"I'm Morgan Graham, usually called 'Curly'."

"Obviously," the driver said with a glance at the crisp brown curls showing under his passenger's white hat. "Machinist's Mate, 2nd Class," he went on as he looked at the rating marks on the Coast Guardsman's blue dress uniform. "You assigned to Oregon Inlet?"

"No, to the Cape Hatteras Life Boat Station."

"Fine! That will make Fatso very happy, especially if you know anything about a duck. He has one that requires the combined services of a mechanic, a wet nurse and a magician to keep it running."

"I know a little about one. Who is Fatso?"

"Chief Bo'sun's Mate Merle Truslow Becker. He believes in God, the Coast Guard, good dogs and the theory that the less he eats, the more weight he gains. This your dog?"

"He sure is. Shake hands, Surfman."

The Chesapeake gravely lifted one paw. Junior Migert bent down and grasped it.

"How do you do, Surfman?" he said cheerfully. "We'll welcome you to the Outer Banks too." He turned to Curly. "Toss your stuff in the bus, and shove it to the rear. We won't leave for an hour yet. I've got to go down the street and do some errands. Care to come along?"

"Why, yes, thank you. I would."

"Might as well get you acquainted in Manteo. It's about the only place off the Banks where you can spend your liberty, unless you go to Norfolk. We'll drop into the *Coastland Times* office. Dick Harrison will be glad to get an item about you. Come on, Surfman, you've got to get acquainted too."

An hour later the Hatteras-Manteo bus, "the only sea-going bus line in the world," according to Junior Migert, rolled along the causeway separating Roanoke Island from the Outer Banks of North Carolina. At Nags Head it turned south and in a half mile the hard road disappeared. Before them

The Outer Banks

stretched a narrow, winding path worn through the loose sand and Curly Graham, sitting in the front end next to the driver, gave an exclamation of surprise.

"You ain't seen nothing yet, Curly," Junior said with a broad grin in which most of the passengers joined. "This is a superhighway compared to what we'll get on the south side of Oregon Inlet."

"There's no road along the Banks?" Curly asked.

"The state highway runs a half mile south of Nags Head as you saw. On the other end, there's a hard road between Hatteras and Avon, that's about seventeen miles, but from Avon north to Oregon Inlet it's just as God made it, or a little worse, for we haven't improved His handiwork by driving across it."

The bus lurched and swayed along the trail—it could hardly be dignified by the name of road—for two miles to the north shore of Oregon Inlet where the state ferry was waiting. During the twenty minute ferry trip Junior introduced the new arrival to the other passengers. They welcomed him cordially to the Outer Banks and invariably the first question asked was as to where he had previously served. When they learned that he was one of the Cape Cod Grahams, a name almost as famous in the Coast Guard annals as Midgett, Scarborough or Meekins, and that he had served two years at the Race Point

Station near Provincetown, their welcome was redoubled. Before the short trip ended, Curly found that he had received two invitations to supper and one to go fishing, in all of which Surfman was included. He quickly sensed, however, that his ready acceptance as a member of the community held a tentative note.

The Outer Banks people were willing to admit that Cape Cod had produced some good surfmen in its time, but the mighty shadow of John Allen Midgett and other local heroes of the surf hung over him and it was by their standards of performance that he would be judged. Nor would Surfman have it all his own way. There were many fine Chesapeakes on the Outer Banks and the owner of each was certain that his dog was the very finest specimen the breed had ever produced.

Curly smiled as he stroked the dog's head. The surf was just as tough at Cape Cod as it was at Cape Hatteras and he was willing to take his chance. As for Surfman—there Curly's mind was at complete ease. All the Chesapeake needed was half a chance and he'd show them. Surfman was, by all odds, the finest specimen that the Chesapeake breed had produced—Curly suddenly laughed aloud as he realized that his thought exactly paralleled that of the other Chesapeake owners for whom he was feeling tolerance, almost pity.

"Going to hit the road, Junior?" the ferry captain asked.

"No, I reckon I'll drive the wash."*

The ferryman spat reflectively over the side.

"Tide's mighty high and coming in fast," he said. "East wind, too."

"That it is," Junior admitted. "Might be I should keep to the upper road, but I'll take a look at the wash anyway. I'd like to drive it as far as Rodanthe anyway. Upper road ain't so tough, there to Avon."

The ferry docked and the bus rolled off and across the sand flats to the point where a pair of ruts led off across the sand wastes. The bus swayed and lurched as though it were about to overturn. Twice, only the driver's quick shift into compound low kept it from stalling in the loose sand. A mile south of the inlet and opposite the Oregon Inlet Life Boat Station, the bus turned sharply to the left and bumped across the low ridge which separated the beach from the higher ground along which the "upper road" wound its way.

The tide was coming in, but there was a stretch of level, hard-packed sand some thirty feet wide left between the ridge and the edge of the surf. Junior swung his bus around and started south along it. His reason for choosing this route was quickly evi-

---
* the packed sand between the line of the surf and the upper edge of the beach, over which the surf washes at high tide.

dent to Curly. The hard sand offered an excellent footing for the bus and the action of the water had made it smooth as a billiard table. The bus picked up speed and rolled merrily along.

As he drove, Junior pointed out to his passenger the wrecks which lay at intervals along the shore, half or more buried in the sand, and told him something of their histories. Some of them, Curly was surprised to find, dated back to the War Between the States (it had been the Civil War at Cape Cod, but Curly quickly learned the difference), although most of them were of more recent origin.

The tide was coming in steadily and several times Junior hesitated as a jutting point forced him to drive through the edge of the water to round it. The wash was getting narrower and it was evidently only a matter of minutes before he would be forced to turn inland and take the upper road, rough as it was.

"If we can get around that next point, we're off to the races," Junior said, pointing ahead to where a spit of sand ran from the ridge into the edge of the surf. "The beach widens out for a few miles south of it."

He speeded up the bus and headed for the shallow water around the point. There was a shower of spray and a cloud of thrown sand as the wheels hit the surf. The bus slewed around, slid off to one side, and came almost to a standstill. For a moment the wheels spun uselessly, then they gripped and the bus lurched forward around the jutting point. As they rounded it, Junior gave a quick exclamation and wrenched his steering wheel to the right. The bus swerved up almost to the ridge, then turned and ran parallel to it for fifty yards before it slowed down to a stop.

"Everybody out!" Junior cried, setting the example by jumping down and running toward the water, Curly and Surfman at his heels.

In the edge of the surf, just south of the point, was a passenger car. Already the lapping waters had buried the wheels to the axle in the sand and with each succeeding wave the car settled a tiny fraction of an inch lower. As they ran forward Curly could feel the ground quiver under his feet, the whole surface shaking like jelly under the pounding of his footsteps. It was perilously close to quicksand, a formation which he was to find later was restricted to a few small areas along the beach.

The only occupants of the car were two middle-aged women and a girl of about six. One of the women was at the wheel of the car while the other woman and the child were pushing valiantly, but uselessly, at the car's bulk.

"Howdy, Miz Green," Junior shouted as he splashed through the surf toward them, the other passengers trailing behind him. "In trouble?"

"That I am, Junior," the woman who had been pushing at the car replied as she straightened up. "And am I ever glad to see you! I reckon as how our troubles are over now."

"I hope they are," the driver replied. "We'll do our best. All right, everybody grab hold," he said as the other passengers came up. "No, Curly, don't try to push it, we must lift and rock it. You're plenty husky, take this front wheel. Now, Miz Olney," he called to the woman at the wheel, "get her in low gear with your clutch out and keep it out until I yell. Miz Green, please get out of the way. Now, fellows, lift and rock her!"

Curly bent his hundred and ninety pounds of bone and muscle to the task before him. Imitating the others, he lifted at his wheel, then let it down as the opposite wheel responded to the efforts of the two men tugging at it. The rocking was kept up for a minute with a steady lift and the car rose slightly from its bedding of sand.

"*Now*, Miz Olney!" Junior shouted.

The car wheels spun as the clutch went in, but, despite the best efforts of the would-be rescuers, the car sank slowly back down into the sand. Curly realized that he was buried to his knees in the soft, sucking sand and it took an effort to free his feet from its stubborn clinging.

"Try it again," Junior said as each man in turn freed his feet and got ready to once more exert his strength. "Lift and rock her!"

Again the car was rocked and lifted. It rose, a fraction of an inch at a time, but when, at Junior's orders, Mrs. Olney applied the power, it sank back deeper than it had been when they had first seen it. The axles were buried completely in the sand and the incoming tide was lapping across the floor boards. A moment later the motor coughed and died.

The men straightened up and looked at the slowly sinking car.

"I knew we'd never get her out thataway," one of them remarked sagely. "Junior, you're going to have to hook on to her and yank her out."

"I'll try," Junior agreed dubiously, "but I've got right poor ground to work on."

He went to the bus and returned with a coil of manila rope. By kneeling down and digging under the axle, Curly managed to fasten one end of the rope to the front bumper bracket while Junior slowly backed the bus down until the other end of the rope could be bent to his rear axle.

"All right, rock her and lift her again," Junior said as he climbed into the bus. "Miz Olney, you get out, we want her as light as possible. Owen, give me a yell when you want me to yank her."

Once more they lifted at the car, straining every muscle. Slowly it came up for an inch, two inches, then it resisted further efforts, sinking back each time it was raised.

"YANK HER!" Owen roared and Surfman barked vociferously.

The rope tightened as Junior let in the clutch of the bus. As it took the strain, the car moved slowly forward, an inch at a time. The men around it lifted with all their strength. Gradually it slid forward for half a car length, then a shower of sand flew out from the spinning wheels of the bus. The big tires had cut through the thin hard surface of the sand and in another moment they had dug in until the axle of the bus rested on the sand. A wave broke around the passenger car and as the water went out, the car settled down again into the sand.

"Well, that did it," Junior exclaimed ruefully as he looked at the bus. "We'll never get her out now without help. Here, Buddy," he turned to a twelve-year-old boy who had been striving manfully to help. "You're the fastest runner here, you high tail it up to Chicamacomico and tell Loman what's happened. Ask him to bring his duck down here on a run with lots of hawser. Hustle up now, make like a rabbit."

"Okay, Junior," the boy replied and sped south along the beach.

"Nothing we can do 'til help gets here," Junior said as he looked with a critical eye at the passenger car, now washed bonnet high by the waves. "If Loman gets here in the next twenty minutes, maybe he can pull her out. If he doesn't, I'm afraid Claudius Olney is going to be in the market for a new car. Let's see if we can do anything about the bus."

Five minutes of straining effort proved that the bus was too heavy and sunk too deeply in the sand to offer any chance of freeing it. They gave up at last and rested their tired muscles while they waited for help. Even Surfman dropped on the sand and let his tongue loll out. He had been an interested spectator and an active helper, if racing around the car and barking encouragement could be construed as helping.

Junior suddenly rose and cupped his ear toward the north.

"There's a car coming on the upper road!" he exclaimed.

With Curly at his side and Surfman bounding up ahead of them he ran across the ridge and toward the winding trail through the sand which was dignified by the name of the upper road. Coming along it was an army command car with two passengers. The driver was a man of enormous girth whose three hundred pounds of weight seemed to overflow the seat of the vehicle. In striking contrast, the passenger was a tall, thin man with a strongly lined face.

"Fatso and Jeff Davis!" Junior cried as he waved to the command car to stop. "We'll be all right now, that command car has four wheel drive and it'll pull anything out."

The car came to a halt and Junior stepped up to it.

"Howdy, Chief; howdy, Mr. MacAlpin," he said. "You're just in time. Claudius Olney's car is out in the surf and about to start for China."

"How come?" the heavy man asked in a deep, rumbling voice.

"Don't ask me, Chief," Junior replied. "I reckon as how Miz Olney figured she was a better driver than she turned out to be. I tried to haul her out and the bus is axle down in the mush."

"Well, we'll see what we can do," Becker said in his deep voice as he let in his clutch and turned the command car toward the beach. He stopped it at the top of the ridge, then climbed out and studied the passenger car which had settled a good deal in the past ten minutes and was starting to list dangerously. "Might be we can haul her out," he said noncommittally as he took a coil of steel cable from the back of the command car. Bend the end of your line to this and we'll try it."

In a few moments the end of the manila rope was

securely fastened to the end of the cable and Becker eased the command car slowly backward until the rope and cable took up the strain.

"Get out there and lift her," his rumbling voice directed.

Led by Junior, the passengers splashed out through the now waist-deep water to the car. They gripped it and at the word of command, strained their muscles in a mighty lift. Becker shifted his transmission to its lowest gear with the four wheel drive connected and let in his clutch. For a moment it was touch and go. The rear wheels of the command car dug into the sand and spun futilely, but the front wheels gripped and, inch by inch, the passenger car moved ahead. Suddenly it rose to the top of the sand and the command car lurched forward. Junior jumped into the car and grabbed the steering wheel. A few moments later the car was out of the water and bumped over the ridge to safety.

"That was swell, Chief!" Junior cried as he unfastened the tow rope. "Now for the bus."

"I'd leave that piece of junk where it is except that it might be a navigation hazard," Becker rumbled. "It's not worth the gas it'll take to drag it out."

Junior grinned and fastened the end of the rope to the front of the bus. A quick pull from the command car and the bus was over the ridge and ready to proceed on its interrupted journey.

"Reckon you'll have to tow Claudius' car to Buxton, Chief," Junior remarked. "It's drowned out."

"Hook her on," Becker assented. "I'll get her there if Miz Olney can steer it."

"That I can, Chief," Mrs. Olney replied. She opened the door and gave a start of surprise. She searched frantically in the car for a minute, then gave a cry of alarm.

"My purse!" she gasped. "It's gone!"

"What sort of purse was it, Miz Olney?" Junior asked as he came quickly forward. "It must be here. Let's look."

"It's a white plastic handbag. It was on the front seat, I'm sure, and it isn't there now."

A quick, but thorough, search of the car proved the handbag was missing.

"It must have been knocked out of the car while we were working on it," Junior said slowly. "I'm afraid it's a gone purse, Miz Olney. It's probably somewhere in the ocean, but we'll never find it."

"But I *must* find it!" Mrs. Olney cried aghast. "It had over two hundred dollars in it; I cashed Claudius' check this morning."

Junior gave a low whistle of dismay, a feeling which was reflected in the faces of the others.

"Come on, let's look for it," Owen cried as he

started toward the surf. "Might be the tide has thrown it up."

They moved along the edge of the surf, searching fruitlessly.

"What color was it?" Curly suddenly asked.

"White. It's a plastic handbag, a fairly big one."

"I wonder could that be it?"

He pointed out to sea. Two hundred yards from shore a white speck was bobbing on the surface of the waves. The bag, instead of being tossed ashore by the incoming tide, had been caught in an outgoing rip engendered by the jutting spit of sand and was moving steadily out to sea.

Mrs. Olney gave a cry of relief, then a fresh gasp of dismay. The bag was in sight, but its recovery, in the absence of a boat, was not an easy problem to solve.

Curly smiled in satisfaction. This was the break for which he had been hoping ever since he had been told of the wonderful Chesapeakes inhabiting the Outer Banks.

"Fetch, Surfman," he said quietly, waving his hand toward the water.

The dog needed no second command. He gave a bark of comprehension and dashed into the edge of the surf. A wave broke around him, threatening to overturn him, but he held his ground. As it receded he followed it, then plunged into the deepening water. A moment later he was swimming sturdily out to sea. For seventy-five yards he swam, raising his head from time to time seeking for the object he had been ordered to retrieve. A bit of driftwood attracted his attention and he swam to it and gripped it in his strong jaws.

"NO!" Curly shouted. "DROP IT! FETCH!"

He waved his arm in an outward motion. Surfman spat out the piece of wood, turned and swam again out to sea. For a hundred yards, a hundred and fifty, he swam, then churned the water for a moment, turned and headed back toward shore.

"NO!" Curly shouted. "FURTHER OUT! FETCH!"

He waved his arm again. Surfman turned obediently and swam sturdily out, his red head bobbing on the surface of the turbulent water. He raised himself with an effort and his eye caught a glimpse of the white speck. He altered his course and a moment later there was a sigh of relief from the spectators on shore. The Chesapeake's jaws had closed on the bag and he was swimming shoreward with powerful strokes of his sturdy legs.

He came to the edge of the surf, made his way through the turbulent boil, stopped and shook himself, then bounded up to his master, the handbag gripped firmly but gently in his powerful jaws. Curly made no offer to take it from him.

"Give it to the lady, Surfman," he said, with a wave of his hand toward Mrs. Olney. The Chesapeake walked over to her, sat down and lifted the bag toward her. She took it from his jaws, then reached down and stroked his wet head.

"Thank you very much—very much indeed," she said. "You're a grand dog and I'm going to buy you a nice piece of meat for a reward."

"ALL ABOA-R-R-D!" came Junior's voice.

The passengers trooped back toward the bus with a congratulatory word to Mrs. Olney, Curly and Surfman bringing up the rear. As they reached the bus, Junior jumped out.

"Curly, you and Surfman might as well ride with Fatso," he said. "It'll save me a two mile detour and I'm way behind schedule. Come on."

He led the way to the command car.

"Chief," he said, "I've got one of your men here. How about taking him aboard and saving me the detour to the station?"

Chief Becker's deepset eyes swept over Curly, who straightened up to an attitude of attention.

"Machinist's Mate, 2nd Class, Morgan Graham reporting, sir," he said formally.

"Glad to have you aboard," Becker replied. "Toss your stuff in the back and climb in. You'll get a rougher ride than you would in the bus, but we'll get you there and with Junior, that's always a gamble. This is Mr. MacAlpin," he went on, motioning toward the passenger as Curly put his luggage in the command car, boosted Surfman in and then climbed in himself. The passenger turned around in the front seat and extended his hand.

"MacAlpin is my name, Jeff Davis MacAlpin," he said gravely. "That is a nice dog you have there."

"Yes, sir, he is. His name is Surfman."

"Surfman? Hm-m-m. An obsolete rating, but one I hope to see eventually restored. And your name is?"

"Graham, sir, Morgan Graham."

"Graham. Hm-m-m. Cape Cod, I presume?"

"Yes, sir, two years at Race Point Station."

"I was not referring to your service, but to your nativity. You are a Cape Cod Graham, I take it?"

"Yes, sir, born and raised at Provincetown."

"And what kin have you on the Outer Banks?"

"None, sir."

"None? Hm-m-m. Of course, it's possible. Quite possible. But—I'm glad to welcome you in my humble way to the Outer Banks. We'll try to demonstrate to you that Cape Hatteras produces as good surfmen as does Cape Cod."

"I'm open to conviction, sir."

"But if you're like most stiff-necked Cape Codders, you'd like to see the man who can convince you. Well, we'll see, we'll see. I would like to talk with you later; with you and your dog."

He turned back and spoke to Chief Becker.

"Merle, if you continue to drive at this rate, you'll save fully five minutes in getting to Buxton. What you will do with those precious moments stolen from eternity I have no idea, but I will spend them and a great many more trying to rest my aged bones from the jolts they are receiving."

"I'm sorry, Jeff," Becker replied with a grin as he reduced the speed of the command car. "I was just trying to keep Miz Olney so busy steering that she wouldn't have time to brood over her troubles."

"And thus give her five additional minutes at Buxton in which to stew around and try to figure out something to say to Claudius when he looks at his car. Your motive is laudable, Merle, but your technique is lamentable."

"All right, Jeff, I'll drive slower."

The command car, despite its lessened speed, swayed and bumped as it went along the rough trail toward Avon where the hard-surfaced road had its start. Curly hung on to the support straps while Surfman braced himself in a corner with all four feet to keep from being tossed in a heap by the bucking car.

Jeff Davis MacAlpin

"I'VE FINISHED with the duck, Chief."

Merle Becker looked up from his overladen desk.

"No one will ever finish with that hybrid freak until it sinks, which will probably be the first time it's launched in moderate surf," he prophesied gloomily. "What was the matter with it this time?"

"Nothing serious. The carburetor was out of adjustment and I had to put in a new set of distributor points. She's running like a clock now."

"And it'll probably run down like a clock as soon as you turn your back on it. Well, it's close to eight bells, so run it into the boathouse and secure for the night. When do you go on tower watch?"

"Not until midnight, Chief. If it's all right with you, I'd like to have four hours liberty this evening."

"Where are you going—Buxton?"

"No, sir, I'd like to go to Mr. MacAlpin's. He

Jeff Davis MacAlpin

asked me and Surfman to come for supper tonight."

"That will be all right," Becker said after a moment of thought. "I always try to oblige Jeff Davis."

"Thank you, sir. Chief, just who *is* Mr. Mac-Alpin?"

"Jeff? I thought everyone knew him. Why, he's the original Jeff Davis MacAlpin, the best newspaper man North Carolina ever produced, except for Josephus Daniels. Jeff has worked on Norfolk and Raleigh papers and most everywhere else. About ten years ago he got badly smashed up in an airplane crash and no one expected him to live, but he did. He was just too ornery to die is the way he explains it. He had to quit working, so he came out here and bought that shack close to the old lighthouse and has been running the Coast Guard ever since."

Curly laughed and Becker's deepset eyes twinkled.

"That's not as much exaggeration as it sounds," he said. "Jeff Davis knows everybody who counts, both in North Carolina and in Washington. Once he makes up his mind to anything, even the Commandant is likely to give up and let him have his way. The lighthouse is a good example."

"The lighthouse?"

"Yes, the old lighthouse. The main reason Jeff came here is that he fell in love with that lighthouse thirty years ago when it was in active use. It almost broke his heart when we had to abandon it and build the steel tower we're using now. He studied the problem and got experts here, then had a C.C.C. camp assigned to work on it. The result was that between barricades and sea oats and one thing and another, they anchored the sand and stopped the wind and the ocean from digging out the foundations. The beach has built back out in front of it again and renovation work has been started on it. New lenses have been ordered and in a few months the light will be moved back into it just like it was in the old days."

"Gee, that'll be fine, Chief."

"It'll save us a lot of time recharging the batteries for the present light every day. Well, that's just one of the things that Jeff has done. I won't tell you the others because he will—that is, if he likes you and starts talking. He knows the history of the Outer Banks and of the Coast Guard from start to finish. and he can give you the history of every wreck that ever happened on the Banks or on Diamond Shoals. Well, go ahead and get policed up. You don't want to keep him waiting."

"Thanks, Chief, I'll be back by eight-thirty or nine."

An hour later, Curly, attired in his dress blues and with Surfman at his side, left the station and started along the road toward the old Cape Hatteras lighthouse. The two-hundred-foot, black and white spirally striped tower stood majestically in the afternoon sun and Curly stopped to admire it.

"No wonder Mr. MacAlpin fell in love with it," he said reflectively. "He really must be quite a guy. I hope he likes me; from what the Chief says he's just the man who could help me, if he wanted to. I've got to go slow, however, but I'll try to get him to talking. SURFMAN!"

He put his fingers to his lips and whistled shrilly. The big Chesapeake, who had ranged over the dunes far ahead of his master, stopped in his tracks and looked back. Curly waved his arm in signal and the dog came bounding toward him. He stopped in front of his master, his head up, waiting for further orders. Curly stopped and rubbed the mahogany head for a moment, then straightened up and swung his arm in signal, indicating a path leading up a low sand hill, on the top of which stood a small white house.

Surfman bounded up the path. As he surmounted the rise he stopped suddenly, his head erect and his ears pricked forward. For a moment he stood poised and motionless, then he moved slowly forward, a step at a time.

Curly followed the dog up the steep rise. As he neared the top, pandemonium broke loose. There was the squall of a cat in a rage, a growl from Surfman, then a howl of pain. Curly bounded up the path just as the door of the cottage opened and Jeff Davis MacAlpin stood framed in the doorway. In the yard before the house Surfman, with deep-throated growls mingled with whimpers of pain, spun about frantically, striving to dislodge a huge cat which clung to his shoulders, all four feet clawing the dog furiously.

The Chesapeake threw himself down and rolled over. The cat sprang aside, but before Surfman could regain his feet, his enemy had returned to the attack, this time digging his claws into the dog's unprotected belly. Surfman twisted quickly, trying to grab the cat. Had he succeeded, one crunch of his powerful jaws would have ended the battle, but the cat was an old seasoned warrior and he eluded the snapping jaws with ease while his long claws methodically raked the dog.

Curly ran to the rescue, but Jeff Davis moved even more quickly. He reached the battling pair and grasped the cat by the scruff of its neck. With a quick lift he freed it from the dog and held it aloft with one hand while he vigorously slapped its ears with the other. Surfman leaped upward to grasp his enemy, but MacAlpin desisted from mauling the cat long enough to give the Chesapeake a resounding slap on the side of his head, diverting the dog's attack. Before Surfman could make a second spring, Curly had him by the collar and was hauling him back.

"Steady, Surfman, down!" he said sharply.

The Chesapeake dropped obediently to a crouch but his gaze was fixed balefully on the cat and a low growl rumbled in his throat.

"Doggone you, Mike," MacAlpin said, dispassionately cuffing the cat vigorously. "One of these days I'm going to slap the ears clean off you. That was a heck of a way to welcome a visitor to our home, such as it is. Now behave yourself!"

He dropped the cat to the ground, but the feline was not yet ready to forego hostilities. He edged cautiously to one side, then with a screech he sprang through the air toward the crouching dog. Surfman was not to be caught napping a second time and he met the attack halfway. He lunged forward, jaws open, but the cat had timed his jump expertly. He hit the ground lightly and leaped to one side, just in time to elude the dog's grasp. In another instant he had leaped into Surfman's back and the battle was rejoined in a bedlam of squalls and growls while tufts of mahogany and grey hair flew through the air.

Curly jumped into the melee, then drew back with a quick exclamation, blood oozing from a line of deep scratches in his hand and wrist. Once more

Surfman threw himself down and rolled to dislodge the clawing feline from his back. The cat jumped free but launched a fresh attack before the Chesapeake could regain his feet. This time Surfman had anticipated such an attack and he rolled quickly over, his jaws seeking his assailant. For a moment it appeared certain that the cat was doomed, but in the nick of time MacAlpin had it again by the scruff of its neck and was holding the squalling, clawing animal aloft.

"Confound it, Mike, I should have let that dog grab you," he said as he slapped the cat's head with renewed vigor. "It would serve you right, you asked for it. Now, *you* behave yourself," he went on to Surfman who was on his feet and seeking earnestly to grab his attacker. At a sharp word from his master, the Chesapeake dropped to a crouch although his teeth were still bared and he was more than willing to resume the battle if opportunity offered.

MacAlpin shook the cat vigorously, then again cuffed the side of its head until it blinked its eyes and strove to squirm free from the grip which held it.

"Now, get out of here before I slap what's left of your ears clean off. If you tackle that dog again, I'm going to let him whale the tar out of you. Clear out of here, Mike, do you understand?"

He once more dropped the cat to the ground. The

feline whirled about to face the crouching dog and for a moment it looked as though the battle would be resumed, but MacAlpin made a quick grab for the cat and Mike leaped to one side to avoid the grasp. He hesitated for a moment, love of battle fighting with discretion, then turned away. The odds were too heavy. With swollen tail and puffed out ruff, Mike moved slowly and with dignity away from the scene of the battle and disappeared around the corner of the house. Surfman growled and tensed his muscles for a spring, but a quick word from his master froze him into immobility. Mac-Alpin gave a dry, twisted smile.

"I wouldn't blame you particularly if you took out after Mike and wore him out, Surfman," he said, stooping down to stroke the dog's curly head. "I didn't know he was around or I would have sequestered him before your arrival. I had to slap his ears off this evening for trying to get too intimate with a robin who's nesting in that tree and he went away in a tantrum. Under those conditions he usually stays away and sulks for a half day or more."

He bent down and examined the scratches on the Chesapeake's back and belly.

"I have some iodine inside if you wish to paint those scratches, Morgan," he said, "although I rather expect they'll heal just as quickly if you let them alone. So far as I know, Mike's claws are not poisonous. I think that all the venom in his makeup has gone into his disposition."

"Oh, Surfman's all right, Mr. MacAlpin," Curly said quickly. "He often gets scratches that deep when he goes into briers. I'm sorry he went after your cat and I don't understand it. Usually he either ignores a cat or makes friends with it."

"He didn't start it, or if he did, Mike met him three-fourths of the way. That cat's disposition is vile, almost as bad as mine is, but we do manage to cohabit on a basis of mutual tolerance. Well, come inside and make yourself at home, or rather, make yourself comfortable. You may drop ashes on the floor here if you wish, which is something you are unable to do at the station without giving Merle an acute case of blind staggers. Do you like fish?"

"Yes, sir, very much."

"I hoped as much. I have half a ham here in case you did not, but it is my belief that I can do things to a bluefish, although the doing requires my close personal attention for a time. Meanwhile, there is Coca-Cola in the ice chest, or beer, if you prefer it."

"Thanks, Mr. MacAlpin, the coke will be fine."

"Suit yourself and if you should get bored by your own company, I can recommend my library to your attention. I will now proceed to cook a fish. Surfman, for your benefit, I will prepare to administer to the necessities of the inner dog at the same time."

He disappeared into the kitchen.

"Can't I help you, Mr. MacAlpin?" Curly called after him.

"No, thank you, Morgan, I prefer to work in solitude. Like many chefs, I choose to hide the secrets of my craft and invite judgment only on my results, not on my procedures. Wait with patience and, I hope, with appetite, until I call you."

Fifteen minutes later he reappeared and summoned his guest.

"Will you ask the blessing, Morgan?" he asked as he bowed his head. "Not that it aids my digestion materially, nor my peace of mind, but I believe in conforming to local custom and in this climate the food does not cool unduly. I think you will enjoy the fish."

Jeff Davis was right, Curly decided after his first bite. There was no question but that he could "do things to a bluefish." The veteran newspaperman ate in silence and Curly, mindful of Merle Becker's words, made no attempt to draw him into conversation. He was glad in a way that he was not called upon to divide his attention but could devote it entirely to the excellently prepared food before him.

"Now I'm going to wash the dishes, Mr. MacAlpin," he said at the end of the meal when he had regretfully declined a third helping of deep dish apple pie.

"You are not," MacAlpin said with an air of finality that admitted of no argument. "The dishes can await my pleasure. I presume, knowing Merle, that you have a limited amount of time available for liberty and I prefer to enjoy your company rather than to profit from the fruits of your labor."

"But I'd like to do it, sir."

"In this house, my young friend, you may speak with truth and not as convention dictates. No one *likes* to wash dishes."

Curly laughed.

"I'm afraid I can't argue with you on that score, sir," he admitted.

"Then why attempt to do so? As a dialectical exercise it would be absurd since the conclusion is already clearly foreseen. Let us engage in lighter and more profitable discourse."

He led the way into the living room, draped his lanky frame over a battered chair, lighted a cigarette and studied his youthful visitor. Surfman moved up close and MacAlpin dropped one hand and absently twisted the Chesapeake's ears. The silence became almost embarrassing before MacAlpin broke it.

"Morgan," he said slowly, "I am a student of Outer Banks history and also, I may add, of human nature. It is within your ability, I believe, to add to my knowledge of both subjects. With your permission, I would like to ask you a few questions."

"Why, of course, Mr. MacAlpin, I'd be glad to have you."

"Some of them—most of them, in fact—will be very personal. You are at perfect liberty to ignore or to decline to answer any or all of them without angering me or forfeiting my liking or respect for you. However, should you choose to answer, I prefer that you tell me the truth."

"Of course, Mr. MacAlpin, I'll be glad to answer. I can't imagine refusing to do so."

"You have not as yet heard the questions."

Jeff Davis MacAlpin lighted a fresh cigarette from the stub of the one he held, leaned back and studied the sturdy form sitting on a chair facing him.

A Matter of History

"Where were you born—and when?" was the first question.

"At Provincetown, sir, on December 3rd, 1929."

MacAlpin made a mental calculation, then nodded.

"That checks," he said quietly. "Have you any brothers or sisters?"

"No, sir."

"Your mother, I take it, never married again?"

A look of bewilderment came over Curly's face.

"No, sir, she didn't," he said slowly. "But how . . ."

His voice trailed off into silence, leaving his question unfinished.

"What is your name?"

"Morgan Graham, sir. I was named after my grandfather."

"A good man to be named after, and an excellent

name to carry. I met your grandfather some twelve years ago when he was on inland flood duty near Louisville and I conceived both admiration and respect for him. Perhaps I might better put my last question in a different form. What was your father's name?"

The look of bewilderment on Curly's face grew and a slight flush of embarrassment mantled his cheeks and brow. He sat silent for a full minute before he replied in a low, hesitant voice.

"I'd rather not answer that question, Mr. Mac-Alpin."

Jeff Davis smoked in silence for a time, then dropped his cigarette in an ashtray and leaned forward.

"I am not trying to force your confidence, Morgan, I am merely inviting it, an invitation you are at perfect liberty to decline. If you prefer, we'll change the subject."

"Let me think, sir."

MacAlpin lighted a fresh cigarette and leaned back in his chair, waiting. Curly's face grew redder as he wrestled with the problem. Suddenly a look of resolution overcame the hesitancy of his expression.

"I'll answer the question, Mr. MacAlpin," he said quietly. "I told you the truth. My name *is* Morgan Graham, my mother resumed her maiden name before I was born. My father's name was—Truslow."

"Surfman Stanton Truslow," MacAlpin said slowly. "Killed in line of duty on March 16th, 1929."

Curly sprang to his feet.

"Killed in line of duty?" he echoed. "Do you *know* that, Mr. MacAlpin?"

"You doubtless mean, can I prove that?" the newspaperman replied. "Unfortunately—no. It is a matter of personal belief, profound conviction, if you prefer that phrase, a conviction based upon my knowledge of the history of the Outer Banks and of human nature. The official record says otherwise."

"It says he deserted the service in the face of danger," Curly said bitterly.

"So it does, but I doubt whether the investigating board which established that finding really believed it in their hearts."

"Then why did they blast his name and record that way—and deny my mother her pension so that she had to live on her father's charity?"

"They had no real choice. They were the prisoners of laws and of regulations. In the face of the established and establishable facts, I can see no other action they could have taken."

"Perhaps—Maybe I don't know all the facts, sir."

MacAlpin rose and went to his book shelves.

A Matter of History

From them he took down two bound volumes and a battered notebook.

"The facts are not too numerous to be rehearsed in detail. First, let us look at the official facts." He opened the first of the bound volumes. "Stanton Truslow held the rating of Surfman, a rating he had earned by nearly seven years of exemplary service in the Coast Guard, all of it on the Outer Banks except one period of eight months when he was temporarily transferred to the Nauset Life Boat Station on Cape Cod. He had been commended once for outstanding service. His record showed no delinquencies and no derelictions of duty.

"On the night of March 16, 1929, he was assigned to patrol the beach, his patrol route running south from the station along the beach in the direction of Hatteras village. It was a nasty night with a wind of gale force blowing from the southeast.

"Two hours after he left the station on his patrol, an emergency call came in which required his services. The usual recall signal, a Coston light on the top of the watch tower, was burned. Without waiting for his return the crew proceeded to the scene of the wreck, taking the surfboat with them. He did not return by the time it was necessary to launch the surfboat and a substitute took his customary place at stroke oar.

"The boat was successfully launched, reached the

wreck and took off the two remaining survivors. Unfortunately, when it returned to the beach, the boat broached to and was overturned. Three of the crew, including the substitute stroke oar, were lost. The survivors of the wreck were saved.

"Truslow still had not returned to the station. This, in itself, could have been readily explainable. He might have been many miles from the station when the recall signal was burned and he might easily have never seen it, the night being what it was. However, he never returned. No one has seen him since, dead or alive, since the time he left the station on beach patrol.

"When he failed to return, his absence was, as a matter of routine, reported. The entire beach between the station and Hatteras village was searched with meticulous care. Everything possible was done to learn where he was or what had happened to him, but there was not the slightest trace to be found. The battered remains of a fishing boat were found high on the beach, but there was nothing to connect its presence with him.

"The Coast Guard authorities, in view of his excellent record, stalled the matter as long as they could, hoping to get some information, but nothing developed. When he remained missing without trace, an investigating board was convened. In view of the official facts, they had no alternative but to

A Matter of History

list him as a deserter and to close his record. So much for the official facts."

"I know all that, sir, but—"

MacAlpin held up a restraining hand.

"Now, let us examine the unofficial facts." He opened the notebook which was filled with entries in his crabbed handwriting. "While stationed at Nauset, he met an unusually attractive girl, the daughter of his station commander. Shortly before he was retransferred to the Outer Banks, they were married and she came here with him. They established a home in Buxton and their complete devotion to one another was a matter of common knowledge. The mere fact that he never returned to her, or communicated with her in any way after his disappearance—I believe that is correct?" He glanced at Curly who nodded emphatically. "That fact alone is, to my mind, entirely conclusive evidence that he did not desert.

"He was in no trouble of any sort; official, personal or financial. He was the third generation of his family who had served with credit, if not especial distinction, in the Lifesaving Service and later, in the Coast Guard. He had generations of tradition behind him. His personal record was excellent. His courage in the face of danger was unquestionable, as shown both by his official record and his local reputation. He had gone up the ladder of rank at a satisfactory rate and was considered to be in line for promotion within a reasonable time."

MacAlpin closed the notebook.

"That about completes my knowledge of the case. From those facts, both the official facts which I obtained from the record and the unofficial facts which I dug up from various sources, I am led to the inevitable conclusion that your father is not, and never was, a deserter."

"I don't believe he was, sir, and neither does my mother."

"No one did at first; not even, I am sure, the board that found him to so be. However, as time passed by, the verdict gradually became accepted and I expect that today anyone you questioned would repeat the finding as a matter of course without thinking to question its accuracy. Such is one of the frailties of human nature. If you repeat any statement often enough, it eventually becomes accepted as a fact, regardless of its improbability. Would you mind telling me, Morgan, why you chose this particular station at which to serve, for I judge from things you have said, that you asked for a transfer here?"

"Mother asked me to, sir."

"The workings of the feminine mind frequently pursue a deviousness of path that puzzles and amazes the mere male."

"Well, you see, sir, Mother never believed that

A Matter of History

Father deserted. She is sure that something happened to him that night and she hoped that, if I came down here, I might be able to find out what it was."

"Is her belief in him shared by others—by your grandfather, for example?"

"No, sir. Grandfather never approved of Mother's marriage—he can't believe that a good surfman could possibly come from any place except Cape Cod—so he was ready to believe the worst about Father. After Father—died, Mother hung on here as long as she could, which wasn't very long. She got no pension, of course, so when her savings were used up, the only thing she could do was to go back to Grandfather. He made it a condition that she resume her maiden name and that, when I was born, I be brought up as a Graham."

"A distinctly Christian attitude."

"He's a mighty fine old man, sir, although he's not exactly what you'd call tolerant."

"He struck me as an unusually stiff-necked old brute when I met him, although his skill and courage were unquestionable."

"I think that later he relented of his attitude, but it would kill him to ever have to admit he was wrong about anything. At least, he has been wonderful to me. He taught me to pull an oar almost before I could lift one."

"Does he ever mention your father?"

"No, sir, I never heard him do so. He brought me up as a Graham and he taught me all about the Graham history in the Lifesaving Service. It's quite a history."

"So it is, but it is no finer than the Truslow history, or those of half a dozen other Outer Banks names."

"Mother always taught me that. I was the only one with whom she could talk about Father and she talked to me about him a great deal. Grandfather brought me up to be another generation of Grahams in the service and to uphold the traditions of the Graham name. Mother, on the other hand, raised me to be a Truslow at heart. I entered the Coast Guard—and came down here—with two objects. The first and foremost is to clear, if I can, my father's name and record."

"That, my young friend, is a laudable ambition and one in which I shall give you any and every assistance which may lie within my power, but I fear I can give you little hope of success. What is your second object in life?"

"I have promised Mother that I will, on my twenty-first birthday, change my name from Graham to Truslow."

"That action should cause no surprise, although it may do so. Even an elementary student of physiognomy, as I am, can see plain evidence of the Truslow blood in you. It was what first roused my suspicions as to your identity. Why does your mother wish you to change your name?"

"She hopes that, even if I can't clear Father's name, I can give honorable enough service that the name Truslow will again be spoken of with respect."

"A second most laudable ambition, although one that seems a trifle unnecessary in view of the respect in which that name is now held, despite the slight blot on its luster that comes from your father's—misfortune."

"What do you suppose happened to him, Mr. MacAlpin?"

"I am afraid, Morgan, that that question will only be answered when the skies shall roll together and the sea shall give up its dead. And now, even at the risk of seeming to unduly speed the parting guest, at what hour are you supposed to return to the station?"

With a startled expression, Curly looked at his wrist watch.

"A quarter after eight!" he exclaimed. "I must be going. I sure thank you, Mr. MacAlpin, for everything you've done. Come, Surfman."

MacAlpin held up a restraining hand.

"One moment, please," he said. "I am a man of peace and I dislike having the serenity of my old age disturbed by the sound of battle. Remain here a moment while I reconnoiter and make certain that my *alter ego*, Mike, still lurks Achilles-like in his tent. If not I shall apply restraint so that my second guest," he stooped and stroked the Chesapeake's head, "may retire in peace although he arrived in tumult."

He stepped out, but a moment later reappeared in the doorway.

"The coast is clear," he announced. "Good night."

"Good night, Mr. MacAlpin. Thanks for the meal and for the information and everything. I'll see you again soon."

"Many times, I hope—both of you."

"Gee, Surfman, it's really late," Curly exclaimed. "We'd better make the run under forced draft."

With Surfman racing down the path ahead of him, Curly stretched out his long legs and headed for the station at a run.

Routine Call

THE TELEPHONE in Chief Becker's office shrilled a summons. For a moment it was silent, then reiterated its demand for attention. Becker's voice rumbled through the station.

"Answer that phone, somebody. I'm in the shower."

Curly dropped the magazine he was reading and hurried to the office.

"Cape Hatteras Life Boat Station, Graham speaking," he announced as he lifted the receiver from its hook.

"Hello, Curly, this is Barron Migert in the tower. Where's the Chief?"

"In the shower."

"Tell him to ring me when he can. We've got a rescue call."

"I'll get him right away."

"Take your time. This is no emergency, just a routine call. The guy's safe enough and it'll do him good to stew awhile."

"Where is he?"

"Stranded on the old *Jason* wreck. He'll keep 'til we get there."

"Okay, Barron, I'll tell him. Hey, hang on a minute, here he comes now."

Becker, still wrestling with his clothes, came into the office. Curly handed him the phone.

"It's Barron in the tower, sir. We've got a rescue call."

"All right, round up the crew and get them ready while I find out what it's all about."

Curly stepped into the hall and pressed a button which sent the clamor of a gong resounding through the station. The Sunday afternoon quiet was broken by the sound of running feet as the station crew answered the summons. A minute later Becker joined them in the locker room.

"Just a routine call," he announced. "A summer bird rowed out to the *Jason* wreck this morning to fish. He didn't tie his boat securely and when the tide started out, the boat went with it. He's jumping up and down on the wreck, yelling bloody murder. We'll have to go out and get him. Better take the dory."

"How about the duck, Chief?" Curly asked.

"Nuts to the duck. It would probably break down before you got half way along the wash."

"No it won't, Chief. I've got that motor running fine and the surf isn't high."

"There's too much ground swell and not enough water where you're going. You'll have to get on the weather side of the *Jason's* bow and drift down on her. You won't find more than a couple of feet under you in the trough and the duck would pound to pieces even if you could maneuver it, which you couldn't."

"I'd like to try it, sir."

"Take the dory. Claudius Olney is out there, standing by with the *Phoebe*. If there was water enough for the duck, he could run in and pick the bird up and we wouldn't have to go out. What's the matter, you afraid of a pulling boat?"

Curly's face grew red as a slow smile spread over the faces of the crew.

"No, sir," he said quietly, choking back with an effort the hotter retort which rose to his lips.

"That's good, take over as cox. Scarsdale, Bassett, Darrow, you're the crew. Don't try to pull the dory on a cradle, just hoist it into the big truck and get going. I want you back as soon as possible, there may be other calls."

"After I pick the man up, shall I go after his boat?" Curly asked.

"No, he rented the boat from Claudius, it's the *Phoebe's* tender in fact, so let Claudius worry about finding it and bringing it in. Move your crew out."

"Yes, sir. Come on, fellows, get the dory off the cradle while I back the truck out. Check her to make sure you have a ring life preserver and a couple of heaving lines."

The three men whom Becker had designated as the dory crew trooped out toward the boathouse while Curly headed for the garage. Surfman met him at the door and gamboled along at his side. When his master opened the cab of the truck, the Chesapeake bounded in without waiting for an invitation.

"Oh, I expect you can go if you want to," Curly said, pausing momentarily to bestow a pat on the dog's head. "But don't make a nuisance of yourself; this trip is strictly business."

Surfman curled up on the seat beside his master while Curly backed the big truck out and drove to the door of the boathouse. In a few moments the men loaded the dory into the truck and clambered aboard.

"All set?" Curly called.

There was a chorus of assent and he put the truck into gear and started along the sandy track toward the Hatteras-Avon highway. About nine miles down the hard road he turned sharply to the left and drove across the sand dunes, breaking his way through the scrubby growth of yaupon and myrtle which clothed them. He bumped over the low ridge which edged the beach and onto the wash. The tide was running out and a wide stretch of dry sand lay between the ridge and the edge of the surf. Half a mile offshore the remains of the freighter *Jason* which had grounded on the Inner Shoals three years before, stood well above the level of the wave crests. Five hundreds yards farther out, a sixty-foot fishing craft was bobbing on the waves.

"There's the *Phoebe*," Basset said, "but I can't see anyone on the *Jason*."

"He's there all right, unless he's jumped over," Curly replied as he shaded his eyes and stared at the wreck. "The seas aren't breaking over it. Well, get that dory off the truck and let's launch her. We want to get back in time for supper."

With an outgoing tide and a moderate surf, the launching of the dory presented no problem to the well-trained crew. In five minutes they were out beyond the line of the breaking surf and were proceeding steadily toward the wreck. From the shore came a long, melancholy howl. Surfman was expressing his keen disappointment at having been left behind.

When his master stopped the truck on the wash, the Chesapeake had bounded from the cab and danced about excitedly on the beach while the dory was being unloaded. As the crew carried the light boat down to the edge of the surf, he had capered about, barking with excitement, but careful not to get in the way or to hinder the crew in their work. When the boat was put in the water and the crew took their places for launching, Surfman jumped into the dory and stationed himself at the bow, fully expecting to go along.

"Out, Surfman!" Curly said sharply. "Come on, get out of that boat."

For a moment the dog could not believe that his master was in earnest, but when the command was repeated sharply, his ears and tail drooped and he got out slowly and retreated to the beach.

"Stay there, Surfman, charge!" Curly commanded.

He gave the command which launched the dory into the surf. The big Chesapeake maintained the crouching position which he had taken at his master's command while the dory went out through the surf, but when it was fairly launched he raised his head to the sky and howled dismally. He rose to his feet and raced down to the edge of the water, his eyes fixed seaward, hoping that his master would relent and signal him to come on.

"There he is!" Curly exclaimed.

His quick eye had caught a movement on the

wreck. The man they were after was still there and he had climbed up onto the stern of the wreck to watch the progress of the dory toward him. Curly rose to his feet and waved his arm in an arc to reassure the man that help was on its way. His action had an unexpected result.

"Here comes your dog, Curly," Scarsdale, who was rowing stroke, said with a grin.

Curly turned about and looked toward the shore with an expression of annoyance. Scarsdale was right. The Chesapeake had been unable to believe that his master really meant the command to stay on shore and had watched intently for the signal which would allow him to take to the water and swim after the dory. When Curly waved his arm in signal to the fisherman marooned on the *Jason*, Surfman interpreted it as being the signal for which he had been hoping. With a joyous bark he plunged into the boiling surf.

In his eagerness he failed to watch the water and gauge the waves as was his wont. The result was that he had gone only a few yards from shore when an incoming wave caught him, whirled him head over heels, swept him up and deposited him on the wash, half strangled. He scrambled to his feet before the back wash of the wave could carry him out to sea and splashed his way through the water until he once more stood on the firm, dry sand.

The second time he profited by the lesson he had learned. He watched the water keenly and when the next wave broke on the sand and started to recede he followed it. At the critical moment, as the next wave broke, he dived into the boiling surf, swimming with mighty strokes toward the dory. For a moment it was touch and go, but his strength and experience triumphed and he bobbed to the surface beyond the breaking wave and swam steadily forward. He was tossed about by the next two waves, then he was out beyond the breaking line of the surf and was making good progress. His red head was moving steadily over the surface of the water when Curly looked back and saw that his order to remain on the shore had been disobeyed.

For a moment he was angry at the dog's disobedience, then his face cleared. After all, he had swung his arm in signal and he could hardly blame the dog for misunderstanding.

"Hold water!" he said.

The crew ceased pulling and held their oars in the water with the blades perpendicular to the keel line. The dory gradually lost way. As it slowed down Curly set a slow stroke which, while it kept the dory with its bow facing the waves, sent it through the water at a snail's pace.

"Boy, oh boy, watch him come!" Darrow exclaimed.

Helped by the action of the outgoing tide, the Chesapeake was rapidly overtaking the slow-moving boat. As he came close, Curly signalled him to come to the stern and as he came alongside, Curly reached down and grasped him by the scruff of his neck and lifted him until he could get his paws over the gunwale of the dory. He reached back and caught the dog by his long tail and lifted. A moment later, Surfman was in the boat, shaking himself vigorously and sending a spray of salt water in all directions.

"Now lie down and behave yourself!" Curly said sternly. As the Chesapeake dropped to a crouch, Curly bent forward.

"Give wa-a-a-y *together!*" he chanted.

The crew took up the new stroke and the dory shot forward through the water toward the wreck.

Mindful of Becker's advice, Curly swung the dory half about and sent it quartering across the waves past the stern of the wreck. The little boat bobbed and danced about on the turbulent water, but as they approached the *Jason*, the wisdom of the Chief's instructions became evident. The strong-running tide was swirling out through Hatteras Inlet and curving north. As it struck the stationary wreck it made a boiling eddy for a few yards, then a strong rip raced seaward on the lea side. It would be extremely difficult to handle the dory in that water, while on the weather side the problem was much simpler. Incoming waves broke against the side of the wreck and made a turbulent, churning seethe of foam, but it was nothing that would give difficulty to an experienced boat crew.

They passed the stern of the wreck and Curly waved his hand in greeting to the fisherman, who had climbed over the battered hulk until he stood on the extreme stern, watching his rescuers approach. He was a man in his early twenties and his deeply bronzed skin and rippling muscles bore testimony to the fact that he was no greenhorn, but a man who had spent much time on the sea or on the beach. He was wearing a pair of bathing trunks and a vivid sport shirt. He waved his arm in reply to the signal from the dory and Curly cupped his hands.

"Go up to the bow!" he shouted. "We'll come down to you on the weather side and pick you up off the bow end!"

He waved his arm to indicate his meaning. A moment later the fisherman's voice came over the turbulent water.

"Okay, Skipper, I'll be there when you are."

He waved his arm again, then stood watching as the dory battled her way through the rough water. It was just west of the wreck that the out-going tide, rounding a small cape to the south, first felt the full effects of the north wind and the little dory tossed and bobbed about like a cork. It took Curly's full attention to keep it steady and going in the right direction. He held to the northern course for a hundred yards, then, with the wreck well to the south of him, he swung the dory's head to the east and made his way seaward until he was opposite the bow of the *Jason*. There he watched and bided his time until he could swing the nose of the dory around to the south and work down toward the wreck.

"Darrow, boat your oars," he called to the bow oarsman. "Stand by with a heaving line."

Darrow raised his oars and boated them, then faced forward, the coil of a heaving line at his feet while the weighted end swung loosely in his hand. The dory, moving with just enough stroke to keep its bow pointed toward the wreck, was drifting steadily down toward the *Jason's* bow. The fisherman, who had watched the handling of the dory with a critical air, waved again to Curly, then started back along the skeleton of the wreck toward the bow which stood well clear of the water. As the dory drifted closer he stood on the edge of the wreck, poised and waiting.

The dory was within twenty yards of the *Jason*. Darrow swung the weighted end of the heaving line in a circle, ready to cast it aboard. The dory rose on the crest of an unusually high wave. As it passed by and the dory sunk into the trough there was a momentary thud and a grating sound as its keel struck the sand which the wind and waves had piled against the wreck. Curly bent his attention to holding the dory on its course for a moment, turning his eyes away from the wreck. As he glanced back, he rose involuntarily to his feet.

"NO!" he shouted. "STAY ABOARD!"

His order was disregarded. The fisherman, who was poised on the edge of the wreck, waved an encouraging hand, then went overboard into the seething surf in a clean, arcing dive. A gasp of dismay came from Curly's lips as the man disappeared into the water, then his voice rang out sharply.

"Give WAY together! Give WAY together!"

The water boiled as the sturdy oars bent under the strain put on them and the dory leaped forward as though endowed with life. In a moment it was alongside the *Jason*, but there was no sign of the fisherman they had set out to rescue. He had cleft the water cleanly, but his head did not appear above the surface.

"Hold water!" Curly barked. "Stern all!"

The dory lost way and lay to, a yard from the wreck, while Curly and Darrow, each with a life preserver in his hand, scanned the water anxiously.

"There he is!" Darrow cried and mingled with his shout came Curly's quick command, "Give WAY together!" Out beyond the wreck an arm had shown momentarily above the surface, only to disappear almost instantly in the boiling rip of the tide which was running rapidly seaward.

The dory shot forward into the tide current and was carried rapidly out to sea. The coxswain and the bow oar scanned the surface intently and Surfman, who had risen from his master's feet and now stood poised with his paws on the gunwale, was watching with equal intentness.

"The darned fool!" Curly raged as he stared at the empty sea. "The undertow's got him and he won't come up for a mile!"

There was an explosive bark mingled with a splash. Surfman was overboard and was swimming out to sea. His quick eye had caught something that neither his master nor Darrow had seen and his instinct, inherited from countless generations of retrieving water dogs, had made his action automatic.

"Surfman!" Curly shouted. "Come back here! Come here, sir! Come here, you mutt, before the undertow takes you under. Surfman, COME!"

The dog churned the water as he strove to turn, but it was too late. A swirl of water caught him and he was sucked down into the seething depths.

"Give WAY together!" Curly shouted frantically as he steered the dory toward the spot where the Chesapeake had disappeared. The boat shot forward, only to lose headway at his next command,

"Hold water!" They were almost at the spot where Surfman had been sucked down and the danger now was that they would overrun him and that he would come to the surface, if he did, behind the dory.

For half a minute the entire crew stared anxiously at the water, then Darrow gave a shout. Only a few yards away the dog's red head broke the surface. Hardly had it appeared before a life preserver sailed through the air to splash into the water a few feet from the dog. Choking and spluttering, Surfman swam toward it, but the dory was moving rapidly. Before the dog could reach the life preserver, the boat was alongside him.

Curly reached out to help him, but before he could grasp the dog's collar, the Chesapeake was caught in another swirling eddy and drawn down beneath the surface. With a shout, Curly leaned over the edge of the boat and plunged his arm into the water. His fingers closed on close-curled hair and he tried to lift. The down drag of the water was too much for his precarious balance. He teetered for a moment, then as the drag of the water grew stronger, he was pulled off balance. Down into the water he plunged, but Scarsdale had seen the coxswain's peril and had acted. His hand caught Curly's ankle in the nick of time. In another moment Curly was hauled back aboard, his fingers still gripping Surfman's ruff.

"You stay aboard, you confounded fool!" Curly admonished the dog as he hauled him over the gunwale, coughing and choking. Surfman shook himself vigorously, then again put his front paws on the gunwale and stared earnestly at the sea.

"There—" Darrow cried, but the rest of his words were lost in Curly's sharp command, "Give WAY together!" as he steered the tossing dory toward the spot, thirty yards away, where a momentary flash of the fisherman's bright shirt had shown above the surface of the water. "NO! he shouted, gripping Surfman by the collar and dragging him back in the nick of time. Undismayed by his former experience, the Chesapeake was about to plunge again into the boiling, eddying water, intent on attempting a rescue.

The man had disappeared again below the surface and the crew held water at Curly's command. Darrow had picked up a boathook and was standing in the bow, hoping to get another glimpse of the bright shirt. It showed again for an instant but was gone before the dory could get close enough to allow Darrow's boathook to reach.

Surfman barked again and Curly had an inspiration. The man was evidently floating close to the surface, and there was no doubt that he was unconscious. He had been under the water for almost ten minutes and throwing a life preserver toward him would be a useless gesture. Experience showed that, even when he was momentarily carried up to where they could get a glimpse of him, he would be sucked under before the dory could be driven close enough for Darrow to catch him with the boathook. It needed someone in the water, someone who could follow the floating body, under the surface if need be, and get hold if it. Yet he dared not allow one of his crew to enter the water. Curly was a powerful swimmer, but he felt that his chances of living in that water would be slight, too slight to warrant the risk. He knew that he was a better swimmer than any other of the crew, that is, any other except—Surfman. Even the dog, powerful swimmer that he was, had been unable to negotiate the water when an eddy caught him, but—

"Come here, Surfman," he said suddenly. "If you want to make a blooming hero of yourself, I'll give you a chance. Come here."

As the Chesapeake crowded closer to his master, Curly quickly bent the end of a heaving line about him, crossing it under his chest like a harness, then securely fastening it.

"Now, watch for him!" he ordered. "Go after him the next time he shows up and if you're sucked under, I can haul you out."

The dory had been steadily running out to sea under the influence of the strong tide, but the rip was losing its force and the boat was gradually slackening its speed. No longer did it toss and bob about so much or so aimlessly, but rose and fell in a steady cadence as the ground swell rolled steadily toward the shore.

For five minutes they watched the surface intently, but unavailingly.

"Pretty hopeless, I'm afraid," Curly said slowly.

Even as he spoke there was a bark from Surfman and the Chesapeake was again in the water and swimming at his best speed.

"Give wa-a-a-y together!" Curly called as he paid out the heaving line attached to the dog. As the dory picked up headway, he swung its bow to follow the Chesapeake. Neither he nor any member of the crew had seen anything, but Surfman evidently had and his actions were the only guide they had.

The dog swam vigorously, ignoring the waves which slapped him in the face and at times momentarily buried him under their surface. Curly kept the dory a boat length behind him while Darrow, boathook held ready, watched anxiously.

"There he is, Curly!" Darrow cried but before the coxswain could give the command to increase the stroke, Surfman had lunged forward and his strongs jaws closed on the arm of the floating man. As they did so, a vagrant eddy swirled near and a wave broke over him. He disappeared, but Curly took in the heaving line steadily and surely. A moment later Surfman's shoulders broke the surface of the water a few feet from the boat. His head was still under the surface, but it was a matter of seconds for Curly to haul him alongside and grip the improvised rope harness.

He heaved up and Surfman's head rose. In his jaws was firmly gripped the arm of the fisherman. Scarsdale boated his oars without command and sprang to Curly's assistance.

"All right, Surfman, let go. *Give!*" Curly commanded as his hand got a grip on the man's arm. The dog released his grip and with Scarsdale's aid, Curly dragged the limp body into the dory. In another moment he had hauled the coughing, choking Chesapeake on board, then bent his attention to giving such first aid as he could to the drowned man.

There was little he could do in the cramped space of the small dory. He knew that he should drain the man's lungs, but when he caught him about the waist and strove to lift him, the only result he achieved was to almost capsize the boat. He looked around in despair to see how far out to sea they had drifted and a cry of thankfulness came from his lips. Less than a quarter of a mile away, the *Phoebe* was slowly moving in their direction. Here was help that was as welcome as it was unexpected. The last time Curly had noticed the actions of the *Phoebe* was when the dory had first been launched. Once it was afloat and started for the wreck, Claudius Olney, sure that the marooned fisherman would now be safe, had turned the *Phoebe* out to sea to search for the boat which had broken loose. It had been found and now the *Phoebe* was returning at a leisurely gait toward Hatteras.

Curly stood up and waved his arms vigorously, then cupped his hands and sent a hail out across the water. Again he waved and the hoot of the *Phoebe's* fog horn answered. The fishing boat swung in the direction of the dory and her engines began to throb as Olney responded to the call.

"Darrow, take oars. Give WAY together! Give WAY together!" Curly cried, abandoning his futile attempts at first aid. The dory shot forward through the water to meet the fishing boat and in a few minutes strong hands lifted the body of the fisherman to the *Phoebe's* deck.

"Come on, Herb."

Followed by Scarsdale, Curly jumped aboard the fishing boat. He and the stroke oar promptly lifted the supine body of the fisherman to drain the water from his lungs. A surprisingly small amount was ejected and they laid the man flat on the deck. While Scarsdale held his head to one side, Curly began to alternately compress and release his lungs, counting rhythmically as he did so.

"How long was he under water?" Olney asked.

"Twenty or thirty minutes, I'd guess."

"Slim chance of bringing him around then."

"Well, we've got to try. Will you take us to Hatteras, Captain?"

"Sure thing."

Without looking up or interrupting the rhythmic pressure he was steadily applying, Curly called out his orders.

"Darrow, Bassett, make the dory fast behind, then come aboard. Secure everything before you leave it."

For fifteen minutes while the fishing boat plowed steadily ahead, Curly kept up his ministrations, shaking his head as others offered to relieve him. There was a faint gasp from the prone figure, a second one, and then faintly and irregularly, the quiescent lungs began to resume their work.

"He's coming around!" Curly cried, watching with the utmost care to make his efforts coincide with those of the man's returning vitality.

"That he is," Olney agreed. "Never reckoned as how he would. What hit him? Looks like he'd been sandbagged."

"He was, by the bottom of the ocean. He went off the *Jason* head first into about two feet of water."

"Wonder he didn't break his neck," Olney said. "But that's why he didn't drown, like as not."

"Could be," Curly assented as he continued his work. "Surfman, get out of the way. You've done your part, now don't make a nuisance of yourself. Go lie down, I told you!"

Surfman, who had been sniffing inquiringly at the prone man, gazed reproachfully at his master, then returned to the rear of the *Phoebe's* deck and dropped to a crouch. A moment later he shook his head vigorously, then, with a quick look at his master, he sat up and began to dig industriously at his ear, striving to free it from salt water.

Old Joey

Merle Becker looked with mild distaste at the bowl of soup which Hooky, the cook, had just placed before him. He sipped experimentally at the brew and the expression of dissatisfaction on his broad face grew more pronounced.

"Why?" he demanded in his deep, rumbling voice, "don't we have some clam chowder once in a while instead of this diluted version of twice-used dish water?"

He glared at Hooky, who shrugged his shoulders.

"No clams, no chowder, Chief," he replied. "There hasn't been a clam brought in here for a month."

"And why no clams?" Becker went on. "Is everyone in this station too lazy to get out and dig a mess?"

"Including the Chief?" Jake Holman asked with a sly grin.

Becker looked hard at his questioner.

"It's not laziness on my part, it's lack of time," he rumbled. "I'm kept too busy going around and waking up men who are sleeping when they are supposed to be painting a boathouse."

A roar of laughter swept the table and Holman's face grew red. Three days before the Chief had caught him taking an unauthorized nap during duty hours and had been publicly reminding him of that fact ever since.

"Okay, Chief, okay, I'll get your clams," he said. "I'll get them this afternoon, if you'll give me liberty and let me have the jeep."

"Where are you planning to get them?"

"The fattest ones are around Oregon Inlet."

Becker thought for a moment.

"When is low tide?" he asked.

"Three-ten today," Herb Scarsdale replied, looking at the tide table posted on the bulletin board.

"If you leave here about twelve-thirty and plan to get back by five, that will give you plenty of time to dig a mess and you can drive the wash both ways. All right, Jake, you can have the jeep."

"Thanks, Chief. Who wants to go?"

"I'd like to," Curly spoke up, "that is, if I can have liberty."

"Go ahead," Becker assented. "Any one else? I can spare one more man this afternoon—for a good cause."

"I'll go," Barron Migert said. "I haven't been clamming for months."

"All right, that does it. Plan to get back here by five. Curly, you'll drive. Come to the office before you leave, I've got a letter I want you to drop off at Chicamacomico on the way."

At twelve-thirty the three clammers were ready. They wore hip boots and each carried a clam fork and a bucket, while Curly had tossed four gunny sacks into the back of the jeep.

"You fellows get in back," Curly directed, "the jeep will ride easier that way. Surfman and I'll ride in front."

The big red Chesapeake needed no other invitation and bounded into the waiting vehicle. Curly paused long enough to rub the dog's head, then let in the clutch and bumped off along the sandy trail leading to the road. As far as Avon they kept on the hard-surfaced road, but when the highway degenerated into two irregular, deep ruts through the sand, Curly turned his steering wheel and sent the jeep bumping across the rough dunes to the hard-packed wash of the beach. The tide was well out and the vehicle made good time along the wide stretch of sand.

They had gone but two miles north of Avon when they saw a solitary figure tramping along the beach.

"That's Old Joey," Holman said. "Let's give him a lift, if he's going far."

The man was tramping steadily along, his eyes fixed on the sand, and it was not until Curly stopped the jeep beside him that he looked up. His face was burned to a deep red by the action of the sun and wind, but it was curiously smooth and unlined, despite the fact that his grey hair and the wrinkled skin of his neck told that his youth, and even his middle age, was long past. His blue eyes had a vacant expression as though his thoughts, if he had any, were miles away from the Outer Banks. He was well muscled and, despite his evident age, he had a look of wiry endurance, but even a casual glance told that his mental development had not kept pace with his physical growth.

"Want a ride, Joey?" Holman asked, leaning out of the jeep.

Joey stared vacantly at the questioner for a moment, then rubbed his hand over his face and head as though he thought that the massage would help his feeble brain to function.

"Going far, Joey?" Holman went on. "We'll give you a ride, if you want one."

"Going far," Joey assented in a mumbling, uncertain voice as though his vocal cords had trouble in obeying the instructions of his brain. "Going to Rodanthe to see Mr. Migert."

"Want a ride?" Holman insisted.

Joey's wandering thoughts seemed to collect themselves and he spoke more clearly.

"Yes, thank you," he said. "I'd like a ride."

"Climb in," Curly said. "Surfman, get in back and make room."

At the sound of Curly's voice, Joey looked up at him. As he stared a curious change came over his face. The vapid expression slowly faded and a look of intelligence came into his vacant eyes.

"Hello," he said in a clear, strong voice. "Where in thunder have you been? I haven't seen you for quite a while."

Curly's face expressed his astonishment at the question.

"Why, I—I've never seen you before," he said.

"Nonsense!" came the clear, strong voice and Joey's blue eyes, now clear and piercing, stared into Curly's. "Where have you been since I saw you last? Have you been away?"

"I just came here a couple of months ago," Curly protested.

"Where from?"

"From Cape Cod."

"I meant yesterday. I looked for you yesterday. I looked for you—yesterday . . . I looked for you . . . I looked . . ."

Joey's voice trailed off into silence. For a full minute he stared intently at Curly, but as he did so the intelligence faded from his eyes and the vacant, unthinking expression he had first worn came slowly back.

"I looked . . . I think . . . I'm sorry." The clear voice degenerated into a half intelligible mumble. "I'm mistaken, please," he said, a note of pleading in his voice. "You won't be angry, please, I meant well. I'd like a ride."

Curly shook his head to clear away the wild thoughts which were chasing one another through his brain.

"Climb in," he repeated his invitation. "Get back, Surfman."

He shoved the Chesapeake out of the way and the old man climbed into the jeep. Curly eyed him keenly, but it was evident that his thoughts had retreated into some faraway place from which they could not readily be recalled. Joey sat silent as the jeep rolled along, his eyes fixed on the sand strip and his hands clasped in his lap. Suddenly Surfman, who found the room he was forced to share with Holman and Migert too cramped to suit him, edged forward. He sniffed inquiringly at the old man for a moment, then his tongue went out in a tentative offer of friendship. Joey's hand went up to the dog's head and he began to fondle him. In another moment Surfman had crowded into the front of the jeep and was pressing up against his new friend. Joey's thoughts came slowly back from their wandering and he petted the dog with interest.

"You're a fine dog, all right," he said in a clear voice, stroking the curly, red head which was pressed against him. "Yes, sir, you're a fine dog. What's your name?"

"Surfman," Curly said.

"Yes, sir, Surfman, you're a fine dog. I had a dog like you once. His name was . . . I can't remember. It must have been—long ago, but I remember him. I don't remember—much," he added in an apologetic tone. "But you're a fine dog, Surfman, a fine dog."

He relapsed into silence and continued fondling the Chesapeake until Curly turned the jeep away from the beach and bumped across the dunes to the Chicamacomico Life Boat Station at Rodanthe. Loman Migert, the officer in charge, came out to greet them.

"Hello, fellows!" he cried. "Hello, Joey, glad to see you."

"Howdy, Mr. Migert," Joey answered as he climbed out of the jeep. His expression was animated, his voice clear and his eyes alert. "There's a mighty fine dog here you should see. He reminds me . . . I can't seem to remember," he said apologetically.

Old Joey

"That's all right, Joey, you'll think of it in a minute," Loman Migert answered heartily. "What can I do for you fellows?"

"We're just going clamming, sir. Mr. Becker asked me to give you this letter."

"Thanks, Graham. Tell him I'll take care of it. Good luck on your clamming."

"Thanks, Mr. Migert, we'll be seeing you."

Curly started to turn the jeep around, but Old Joey stepped close to it.

"Thank you for the ride," he said. "You must come fishing with me one of these days. I think I'll be able to get you some . . . some . . . Come fishing with me some day. Goodbye, Surfman, you come too."

"Who on earth is that character?" Curly asked as he swung the jeep north on the wash and started toward Oregon Inlet.

"Old Joey?" Holman answered. "Oh, he's just Old Joey, a fisherman who lives in Avon. I don't know who he is, but he's the best fisherman around here and if you go out with him, you'll get fish. He doesn't go out very often, just when he feels like it or needs to pick up a few bucks. The rest of the time he just loafs, or does odd jobs for anyone who needs help. Most of the time he won't take any pay for his work."

"He seems—well, peculiar."

"Yeah, he's a queer duck. Most times he's okay, acts and talks just like anybody, but sometimes he's just a dimwit. I never saw him quite as bad as he was today. Could be he's getting worse. He thought he knew you."

"Yes—he did."

"He gets screwball ideas like that sometimes, but there's no harm in him. He never hurts anyone. I'll tell you, ask your pal, Jeff Davis, about him. He's more likely to be able to give you the lowdown on Joey than anyone else. What Jeff Davis doesn't know about this country isn't worth knowing."

"Thanks, I think I'll ask him. Where do we turn off to the Sound?"

"Not for a couple of miles yet. I'll tell you when."

Curly relapsed into silence as he drove along, but his thoughts were busy. He had come to the Outer Banks to try to solve one mystery and here was a second one staring him in the face. Of course, there could be no possible connection between the two, and yet . . . He resolved to seek counsel of Jeff Davis MacAlpin at the first opportunity.

His chance came that night when Becker asked him to take a peck of the clams they had dug to the newspaperman.

"Joey," MacAlpin said in response to Curly's question, "is a castaway. In that respect, he is no different from most of the Outer Banks people, or rather, of their ancestors. The Banks were first settled by castaways. Wrecks were quite numerous in the sailing days, and not all of them were due solely to the stress of the weather. Nags Head acquired its name from a custom of the early inhabitants. On thick, stormy nights, they would tie a lantern to an old nag's head and drive her back and forth along the beach. The bobbing of the light would, to a man at sea, resemble the motion of a buoy light and many ships were thus lured on shore, to the enrichment of the Nagsheaders. It was not until the federal government cracked down that the custom faded. The fading was aided by the fact that they found it was pecuniarily more profitable to take a regular salary from the government for saving life than to rely on their former precarious means of livelihood, although to this day, I wouldn't trust an Outer Banks man aboard a wreck, if I wanted it preserved in *status quo* with all removable fittings left intact."

"But about Old Joey—" Curly said, but MacAlpin was started on his favorite topic and would not be denied.

"One of the most interesting wrecks that occurred was that of a shipload of fine Arabian horses. Many of the horses got safely ashore and with them came two Egyptians who had been caring for them on the trip. It was from these purebred Arabian horses that the strain of so-called 'Outer Banks ponies' developed. At one time all of the Outer Banks islands had wild herds of them, but they were gradually captured or killed off until today, only a few scattered bands remain, and they bear the brands of ownership.

"The two attendants remained on the Outer Banks and affiliated with the local population. One of them was named Pharaoh, or at least, was so called. The other had an unpronounceable name and was designated simply as 'that Arab'. To this day there are distinct traces of Egyptian blood in many of the Banks families and the names 'Farrow' and 'Wahab' are quite common, especially as middle names."

"But about Joey—"

"Morgan, your impatience in attempting to abridge my learned dissertation on matters of historical interest is reprehensible, but the impetuosity of youth cannot be denied. Joey is a modern castaway and, like many other things, the facts about him are more shrouded in mystery than is the case with happenings of earlier years. I am sorry, but I can not tell you the name of the vessel from which he was stranded.

"Some twenty or so years ago, rumors of a wild man, living hermit fashion in the woods near Frisco, became common. He seemed to do no harm, although some petty thievery was laid, possibly with some justice, at his door. He molested no one, however, and was seldom seen.

"This situation went on for some months until one day he was found by two boys who were hunting. He was unconscious and lying in a crude shelter he had constructed. The boys brought word to Buxton and a rescue party went out and brought him in, more dead than alive. There was no doctor on the Outer Banks, which probably accounts for his survival. Be that as it may, he eventually recovered his physical health.

"He remained for a time at Buxton, then he drifted over to Avon and there, for the past eighteen years, he has remained. He is an excellent fisherman and could, doubtless, have acquired a moderate degree of worldly wealth, by Outer Banks standards, had he chosen to exert himself. Instead he has contented himself with the ownership of the shack where he lives, plus his boat and nets. He works when he pleases at occupations which he enjoys. He is fond of animals. He happens to honor me by his friendship and when he is at Buxton, he invariably shares my rooftree with me for a night. That, I believe, is the full extent of my knowledge about him."

"Surfman took to him at once."

"That is not surprising," MacAlpin said, pulling the ears of the Chesapeake who was sitting beside him. "Surfman has the makings of a true philosopher in his disposition and he doubtless recognized a kindred spirit. Given an opportunity, the two will probably become firm friends."

"One funny thing, Mr. MacAlpin, when he first looked at me, he thought he knew me and wanted to know where I had been, because he had been looking for me."

"That has happened before with others. I believe his mental illness to be either the result of an accident or caused by his prolonged sickness when he was first found. When he began to gain health, he was questioned extensively by members of the community. At first he would simply stare blankly at his questioners, but as he grew stronger, he became in a measure, articulate. Gradually he' improved until today, most of the time a casual questioner would notice nothing unusual in his manner of talking or in the coherency or continuity of his thoughts.

"At times he relapses into a semi-moronic state, in which I judge he was today, from your description of his behavior. On the other hand, at times he gets a flash of normalcy, usually as the result of a mental shock. A number of times some person or object, or even a casual phrase, has evidently given him a shock that seemed momentarily to promise a return of his memory, but such flashes are brief and they fade away before he can marshal his thoughts to a sufficient extent to express himself connectedly. Such flashes are usually followed by a period of depression, of less than his normal mental activity."

"Couldn't people have checked the wrecks that happened at the time he came ashore and traced him?"

"Such attempts were made, but since no one could say within a matter of several months just when he came ashore, they were not successful. No, Morgan, I am afraid that the question of Old Joey's identity will remain one of the unsolved mysteries of the Outer Banks."

"I see," Curly answered thoughtfully. "When he seemed to know me, I hoped for a moment that I had found a clue—"

"I'm afraid not. Your idea is not entirely original with you, for I looked carefully into the matter of relative dates several years ago. Joey was not reported until four or five months after your father disappeared—and there is not the slightest trace of physical resemblance between them."

Curly flushed.

"I didn't mean I thought they might be the same, sir."

"Yet, even that possibility could not be ignored until it had been explored thoroughly."

"I suppose so. He asked me to go fishing with him."

"An invitation which I would accept, the more so that it is one that is seldom extended. Our friend, Joey, prefers, as a general thing, to fish alone. He has a small, but sound boat, with an excellent motor and he keeps his equipment in good shape. You will find him an excellent fisherman who knows the waters here as few do."

"I think I'll go with him, sir. It's just possible he might remember something."

"The irrepressible and unreasoning optimism of youth," MacAlpin replied with a dry smile.

"I've got to go now, sir. I go on tower watch in an hour."

"That is my loss for it deprives me of your company. Please convey my thanks to Chief Becker for his kindness in remembering my appetite for bivalves."

"That I'll do, Mr. MacAlpin, and thanks for the information you gave me. Come on, Surfman."

The Chesapeake rose promptly and came to his master's side. From behind the kitchen door came an angry squall and Surfman's ruff rose as he stared at the closed door.

"Mike is expressing his resentment at having been placed in durance vile for the period of your visit," MacAlpin observed. "But it is for his spiritual welfare. His spirit needs chastening. Good night."

"Good night, Mr. MacAlpin."

Curly's thoughts were busy as he walked along the trail toward the station.

"Of course, Mr. MacAlpin is right," he mused. "He knows all about this place and everyone in it, but still, at the same time . . . Joey certainly thought he knew me. Of course, that doesn't mean a thing, Mr. MacAlpin says, but . . . Surfman, I think we'll take up that invitation the next liberty we get and go fishing. How about it, Dog, you willing?"

Surfman looked up at his master and wagged his tail.

Tower Watch

"How soon will you finish that job?"

"Oh, hello, Chief, it's you. I thought a cloud had gone over the sun, it got so dark in here."

Merle Becker ignored the reference to his bulk and crossed the boat house to where Curly was working on the engine of the motor surfboat. He stooped to stroke Surfman's head as the big Chesapeake came forward to greet him.

"How soon will you finish that job?" he repeated.

Curly scratched his head and looked speculatively at the parts of the motor laid in orderly fashion on a canvas paulin.

"Unless I find something more, there's about two days work left to do on it," he said. "It hadn't been worked on for some time and I had to give it a complete overhaul."

"It should be ready for test tomorrow night then."

"Not before Friday noon at the earliest, Chief. I'm on tower watch from noon 'til four o'clock this week, and that gives me only mornings to work on it."

"That you are," Becker assented. "I'd forgotten that. I wonder if I couldn't shift the schedule around some way. I'd have to put Herb on double watch if I did."

"I can work on this motor evenings after I come off watch, Chief, if it's that important. I didn't realize it was a rush job, I thought it was just a routine overhaul."

"That's what I planned, but Mr. Hargrove called up a few minutes ago and I've got to send our motor launch to Oregon Inlet for a week. With it gone and the motor surfboat laid up for repairs, we haven't anything to send out on a rescue call but the dory and the pulling surfboat."

"We've got the duck standing by, Chief."

"That piece of junk!" The expression of Becker's voice was eloquent.

"There's nothing the matter with the duck, Chief. I've got her in first class shape and I'll trust her in anything the motor surfboat will go through."

"I wouldn't," Becker grunted. "I'll feel lots safer when you have that job ready for the water."

"Shall I work on it this afternoon instead of standing tower watch?"

"No, you'll have to stand your watch today, Herb's on liberty. I'll see what I can do to shift the schedule tomorrow."

"Okay, Chief, I'll push the job all I can, and I'll put in a couple of hours after supper tonight."

"I'll appreciate that, Curly. Surfman, see that he keeps busy and doesn't loaf on the job."

Curly laughed.

"Surfman really stands guard so he can wake me up when he sees you coming," he countered. "I'll push her along, Chief, but you don't need to worry as long as we have the duck."

"Nuts to the duck," Becker rumbled as he strode away.

"The Chief sure doesn't trust the duck, Surfman," Curly said as he turned to his work. "We do, don't we, old fellow? We learned at Race Point how one should be used. Not that I wish anyone any bad luck, but I'd really like to see a call come in where we had to use it. There won't be one, though. Things like that just don't happen."

At eleven, Curly laid aside his tools and crossed to the main station building where he cleaned up for the noon meal. At twelve, with Surfman at his heels, he climbed the watch tower and relieved Holman, who had been on watch during the morning hours.

His first task was to check the log and enter on it

the fact of his relief. There were only routine entries for the previous watch, he noted. Holman had had an uneventful four hours of duty. He next checked the radio and found all channels clear and operating correctly. He entered on the log the temperature, the direction and velocity of the wind, and reported the surf as "moderate." He next checked the telephone circuits to Hatteras village, Little Kinnakeet, Chicamacomico, Oregon Inlet, Manteo and Virginia Beach, from where he could be quickly connected with the District Headquarters at Norfolk and the Air Station at Elizabeth City. Everything was in perfect order and he took the binoculars from the rack and went outside to the platform surrounding the tower. The visibility was unlimited and the Diamond Shoals lightship, thirteen miles away, could be plainly seen on the horizon. A few miles closer, near the outer edge of Diamond Shoals, another ship was anchored.

"Still trying to salvage the *Otomie*," Curly said as he studied the anchored ship. "I wouldn't think they could do much diving with so heavy a ground swell running. At that, I reckon it's calm enough thirty fathoms down. All the same, I'm glad I'm not a diver, aren't you, Surfman?"

Surfman looked inquiringly at his master and wagged his tail. Curly swept the horizon with the glasses, then went inside the tower and replaced them in the rack. There was nothing to do and he sat down where he could watch the water, resigning himself to an uneventful and tiring four hours on watch.

The time passed slowly and with deadly monotony. At half hour intervals Curly would rise and punch the key on his watchman's clock, evidence that he had stayed at his post and kept awake during his tour of duty. Aside from this act and a perfunctory sweep of the empty waters with the binoculars at frequent intervals, there was nothing to do. On Curly's first few trips out to the platform Surfman accompanied him, but he was as bored as his master and eventually he curled himself up and went to sleep, merely opening one eye and giving a lazy thump of his tail when Curly rose and moved about. A few routine messages came in over the radio, but nothing for the Cape Hatteras Station and nothing requiring recording in the log book.

"Four bells," Curly remarked as he made the two o'clock punch on the clock. "Half over, thanks be! I wish something exciting would happen."

He had hardly spoken when the radio broke its silence.

"Nan Mike Nan Eight Seven"* came in strident tones from the speaker. "This is Nan Mike Dog

---
*The phonetic alphabet. See Appendix III

Sugar. Nine Mike Nan Eight Seven, this is Nan Mike Dog Sugar. Over."

Curly grasped the microphone and pressed the sending button.

"Nan Mike Dog Sugar, this is Nan Mike Nan Eight Seven," he said. "Eight Seven to Dog Sugar. I read you loud and clear, loud and clear. Over."

"Dog Sugar to Eight Seven," came the reply. "Your signals loud and clear. The *Jonas K. Bell*, Baker Easy Love Love, *Bell*, the salvage ship operating on the edge of Diamond Shoals, reports they have a diver in very serious condition. His line became fouled and they had to send another man down to untangle it. When they got him up, he seemed to be all right, but now he has developed a severe case of the bends and needs to go into a recompression chamber as soon as possible. Have you read this? Have you read this? Over."

"Eight Seven to Dog Sugar. I read your message. Go ahead, please. Over."

"Dog Sugar to Eight Seven. The *Bell* can't leave her anchorage and her tender is away, so they want us to take care of the matter. We called Norfolk and a plane is coming from Elizabeth City, but I don't think they will be able to land. There is a very heavy ground swell out here. District said to alert you and have you stand by to take him off if the plane can't handle it. Have you read this? Over."

"Eight Seven to Dog Sugar. I read your message. We will stand by. We will stand by. Over."

"Dog Sugar to Eight Seven. Roger. Roger and out."

Curly replaced the microphone on its hook, inserted a jack in the telephone switchboard and repeated the message from the Diamond Shoals lightship to the Chief. A few moments later Becker puffed his way up the stairs and into the tower.

"There comes the plane, Chief," Curly said, handing his superior the binoculars. Far to the north a tiny speck had appeared in the sky. It grew rapidly larger as the plane approached.

"That can't be our plane," Becker grunted as he leveled the binoculars. "They couldn't get here that soon."

"It's a PBY, a Catalina," Curly said.

"You're right, Curly, it *is* a Coast Guard plane, no question about it. It must have been out on patrol right close to here when the call came through. Let's see what they can do."

The two men watched as the big Catalina came nearer. It passed almost over the watch tower and dipped its wings in greeting as it did so, then turned out to sea toward Diamond Shoals. Over the *Jonas K. Bell* the plane circled three or four times, then sloped down toward the surface of the water. Lower and lower it dipped, but just before it met the surface it leveled off, then zoomed upward and once more swung in a wide circle about the anchored ship.

"He doesn't like the looks of the water," Becker rumbled. "Don't know as I blame him much. There he goes down again."

A second and then a third time the plane swooped down, but each time before its hull touched the water it leveled off and began to climb. As it started to climb the last time, the radio in the tower spoke raucously.

"Nan Mike Nan Eight Seven, this is Nan Mike Zebra King," it said. "Nan Mike Nan Eight Seven, this is Nan Mike Zebra King. Over."

"That's the plane talking," Curly exclaimed as he picked up the microphone. "Nan Mike Zebra King, this is Nan Mike Nan Eight Seven. Eight Seven to Zebra King. I read you loud and clear, loud and clear. Over."

"Zebra King to Eight Seven. Your signals clear. The cross swell out here is so bad that I'd probably crack up if I tried to light. What is the condition of the beach north of the old lighthouse? Is it in shape for a landing? Over."

"What on earth is he talking about?" Curly demanded. "Has he gone completely nuts?" He spoke into the microphone. "Eight Seven to Zebra King. The tide is out and the beach north of the old lighthouse is wide, hard and dry. Dog Roger Yoke. Dry.

There's no water on the beach. You can't land on the beach. Over."

"Zebra King to Eight Seven. Keep your shirt on, Sonny, I'm not going to land. There's a JRF* on the way from Elizabeth City and due here soon. Can it land on the beach? Can it land on the beach? Over."

"Eight Seven to Zebra King. Yes a JRF can land on the beach, it can land on the beach. Over."

"Zebra King to Eight Seven. That's fine. Get men out with flags to inspect for driftwood and to mark a landing runway. Send a boat to the *Jonas K. Bell* to bring the casualty to shore and the Goose will pick him up. Do you read my message? Over."

Curly looked at Becker, who nodded.

"Eight Seven to Zebra King. I read your message. Wilco. Roger and out."

"Hey, wait a minute!" Becker exclaimed. "That won't work. Our motor surfboat is laid up and our other boat is at Oregon Inlet on the Sound side. It will take four hours, nearer five, for it to get here and then out to the *Bell*."

"We've got the duck."

Becker gulped.

"In that surf?"

"Sure thing, Chief, that surf isn't too bad. I'll take her out—and bring her back."

Becker hesitated only a moment.

---

* a Grumman Goose, an amphibious plane.

"It's an emergency," he said, "and we've got to take a chance. Go ahead and take her out. You're the only experienced duck driver we have, so it's your baby. Pick up two men with flags, the cook will have to be one, and take them to the beach to mark a landing strip for the plane. Take two men with you in the duck. That will strip the station clean."

"What about the tower watch, Chief? I can make out all right with one man in the duck, if it's necessary."

"Take two, I'll take over the tower watch myself. It's about all I'm good for," Becker went on with a lugubrious glance at his bulging waist line. "I'll have to stay up here anyway, to keep in touch with things."

"Yes, sir. Come on, Surfman."

"Wait a minute, Curly. After you drop those men on the beach, drive the highway to Hatteras village and take the water there. That will give you deep water for launching and you'll have it fairly calm in Hatteras Inlet. Come back the same route."

For a moment Curly hesitated as though about to argue the Chief's order, then he shrugged his shoulders.

"Okay, Chief," he said. "I'm on my way."

He ran down the stairs of the watch tower, Surfman at his heels. A moment later the alarm gong was calling all hands to the locker room.

The Duck Goes Out

IN A FEW TERSE WORDS, Curly explained the situation.

"Wyman, you and the garbage mangler get white signal flags for the beach. Barron and Jake will go with me. Get blankets, a litter, and plenty of spare line. Meet me at the duck."

With Surfman at his heels, he ran to the open shed where the duck was parked and started to strip off the canvas covers which protected the amphibious vehicle from the weather. As soon as he had the cab uncovered, he started the motor to warm it up. By the time Holman and Migert joined him and loaded the equipment they had brought, the duck was ready to move.

Curly was sorely tempted to head straight for the beach, but there had been recent rains and some of the ground between the station and the beach was pretty soft and soggy. While he felt certain that the six wheels of the amphibian would enable it to make its way through almost anything, the thought that Becker was watching from the tower had a sobering influence. This was the first time the Chief had allowed him to take the duck out on a rescue mission and it behooved him to take no chances. He backed the vehicle around and started down the trail leading to the old lighthouse.

Once on the wash, he drove north for a quarter of a mile, watching the sand closely. Twice he stopped for a moment while the men picked up and carried back pieces of driftwood which might possibly have interfered with the landing of the expected plane.

"This is far enough," he decided. "Drop off here, Wyman. I'll turn around and take Hooky back past the lighthouse."

Ballard jumped out, white signal flag in hand, and Curly backed around and retraced his course. He went well past the old lighthouse, making certain that the beach was level and clear from debris. When the distance between him and the spot where he had left Ballard was twice the space the Goose would need for a landing, he stopped again.

"Okay, Hooky," he said to the cook. "Get out here and watch for the plane. You know the signals, don't you?"

"Sure thing."

The cook jumped down and Curly started ahead.

The wash was wide and hard and he was sure he could make better time by driving it as far as Frisco where the Hatteras-Avon highway would be only a few yards away across the dunes than he could by retracing his path to the old lighthouse and then following the sand trail to the highway.

At the point of Cape Hatteras he stopped the duck and studied the sea. Becker's orders had been clear. He was to follow the Hatteras-Avon highway to Hatteras village on Pamlico Sound and take to the water there. That would mean that he would enter comparatively calm water and the surf *was* high, much higher as seen from the level of the breakers than it had appeared from the elevation of the watch tower and at a distance of half a mile. On the other hand . . .

Curly made a rapid calculation. The *Jonas K. Bell* was anchored at the edge of Diamond Shoals, only a few miles off shore. He was now at the closest point he would be to it, for a trip along the highway would take him constantly farther away from his eventual goal. While he could cover the land miles quickly, every mile he drove would have to be added to the water trip and a duck, even if pushed, could not make much more than six knots.

If he entered the water here, he would be lying alonside the *Bell* in an hour, or an hour and a half at worst. If he followed Becker's orders, it would take him at least fifteen minutes to get to Hatteras. When he entered the water of the sound, he would have a boat trip of at least an hour before he would round the point of the island and get through Hatteras Inlet to the open sea. Even when he had done this, he would still be twice as far from the *Bell* as he was now, maybe nearer three times as far, he thought as he visualized the map of the Outer Banks. Such a trip would consume four hours and if the diver on the *Bell* was in as critical a shape as the message from the Diamond Shoals lightship had indicated, every minute counted. Of course, orders were orders, but . . . Curly suddenly made up his mind.

"Put on life preservers," he said tersely, setting the example by starting to unfasten the one lashed by the driver's seat.

"Going in here, Curly?" Barron Migert asked in a voice that quavered slightly despite his efforts to speak in a casual tone.

Curly gave him a quick glance. Migert was pale, but he was unlashing a life preserver with steady fingers. Holman, his back to Curly, was similarly occupied.

"Yes, I am," Curly said. "I can save two or three hours by launching here instead of at Hatteras and the trip through rough water will be much shorter. Toss me an extra preserver, will you? I want to put one on Surfman."

He fastened the life preserver about the Chesapeake's sturdy body, then glanced back.

"All set?" he asked.

"All set," Holman and Migert chorused.

"Here we go, then," Curly said as he faced the duck toward the surf and engaged the clutch. "I'll bet the Chief is having a litter of kittens right up in the tower."

He grinned at the expression he could imagine was on Becker's face, then gave his attention to the task at hand.

He slowly edged the duck down until it was at the edge of the surf with the water curling up to within inches of the front wheels. There he stopped it and studied the incoming waves. They were running in a pattern of five and he waited until two complete cycles had rolled in and broken. As the last wave of the second cycle started out, the motor of the duck roared and the vehicle moved forward, following the retreating wave down the sand. A moment later the front wheels were churning up the sand and Curly pressed his gas pedal to the floorboards.

The duck charged ahead into the surf. The first wave of the next cycle broke on the bow and tossed spray high over the cab and into the body. The duck shuddered at the impact, but it forged steadily ahead and a moment later the front wheels lifted slightly. The second wave came charging in and the duck was waterborne. It swayed as though about to broach to, but Curly already had the propeller spinning and as the wave rolled past the blades bit water. The duck wallowed about in an ungainly manner but she swung around till her head was straight into the incoming waves.

It seemed to barely move and for a moment Curly felt his stomach sink, but as the third wave lifted, the propeller caught hold and when the duck dropped into the wave trough, she began to move steadily ahead. When the last wave of the cycle smote her on the bow, she merely seemed to shake as though throwing off the weight of water that poured over her and before the next cycle could run in, she was beyond the line of breaking surf and was proceeding steadily seaward.

"Did she ship much water?" Curly called back.

"Not too much. The bilge pump is spouting steady, but I don't think there's more than a couple of inches aboard."

"That's good, but hang on to your shirts. It'll probably be worse going over the inner shoals."

The duck forged steadily ahead, coming momentarily closer to the line of breaking surf that marked the offshore bar. The surf was higher than it had been on the beach and for a moment Curly hesitated. It looked bad—very bad. Possibly he had made a mistake in entering the water where he had. Maybe it would be the part of wisdom to turn around—that is, if he could make a turnaround in the restricted space he had to work in without broaching to—and head back for the beach. He was certain that he could land safely and if he took to the water at Hatteras he could go out through the inlet and not have this peril to face. Still, an attempt to turn around might be almost as dangerous as going ahead. Also, such a maneuver would waste a lot of valuable time.

"It's probably too late to turn back anyway," he decided as he looked at the line of breakers only a few yards ahead. "Brace yourself, Surfman, here we go!"

He slowed the duck, waiting his chance. It came in a minute and he drove the amphibian straight forward into the seething water.

The first wave struck the duck with a terrific impact, pouring tons of water over the bow and against the windshield. The amphibian shuddered and slowed almost to a stop, then caught headway again. She rose and seemed to toss off the water with a shrug as she lunged into the second wave.

Again she was almost buried under the churning

water, but she rose slowly and sluggishly and drove doggedly ahead.

"If she weathers the next one—" Curly grated through set teeth as he wrestled with the wheel.

The third wave struck the duck head on and for a moment the amphibian wavered. Curly held his breath. Then slowly she rose and the wave passed by her and not over her. As the wave passed there was a sickening thud as her keel grounded on the shoal. The duck rose slightly, struck again, and then as the fourth wave came in, she was lifted high on its crest and her propeller sent her steadily forward. Curly let out his breath with an explosive gasp. Two hundred yards of rough and seething water lay ahead of him and probably some of it was even shallower than the bit he had just passed over. On the other hand the bilge pump was steadily lightening the vessel and he felt that the worst was over.

He dared not relax his vigilance for an instant, but hung on to the wheel with a tight grasp, careful to keep the nose of the duck headed straight into the waves. It would take very little quartering to cause the amphibian to broach to in this water, and if such a thing were to happen . . . Curly shook his head. That was something he shouldn't think about—the navigation needed all of his attention.

The far edge of the shoal approached. Here the

water was boiling and seething with greater force. Curly slowed the propeller with a silent prayer and watched his chance. There was a momentary lull and he gunned the motor. The amphibian shot forward with a lurch. There was a sickening thud, a second and a third as they grounded. Then a swell caught them and lifted them and the duck slid forward over the bar and was floating again in deep water.

Curly sighed with relief and took one hand from the wheel long enough to give a reassuring wave to the two members of the crew. The worst was definitely over. The trip out to the anchored *Jonas K. Bell* would be a simple matter. It could be dangerous enough if he should get careless and relax his vigilance, but it would be nothing to what they had just been through.

Forty-five minutes later Holman and Migert caught the heaving lines cast from the deck of the *Bell* and hauled aboard hawsers which they whipped around cleats on the duck's deck. The water was rough and turbulent, but they were securely fastened to the *Bell* and rose and fell with her.

"How's the patient?" Curly asked.

"He's in pretty bad shape," the Master of the *Bell* answered. "He needs to be got into a recompression chamber as soon as possible."

"Don't you have one on board?"

"Yes, but my compressor went bad yesterday. My

tender has it on shore now being repaired."

"I see. We'll have him on shore in an hour and there'll be a plane waiting to fly him to Norfolk."

"Yeah, I saw a plane land near the lighthouse about twenty minutes ago. How are you going to take him aboard?"

"We'll pass up a boat litter. Wrap him in blankets, put him on the litter and lash him down. Then lash life preservers to each corner of the litter so it will float right side up."

"What's that for, you aren't going to tow him?" the Master exclaimed.

"Oh, no, we're taking him on board, but we've got some fairly rough water to go through on the way in."

"I see."

"When you have him ready, lower him with your boat falls so he'll come down to us level. We'll take it from there."

"Right, Captain. Bring Joe topside. A couple of you grab that litter."

Five minutes later the groaning diver, swathed in blankets and lashed to the litter, was gently lowered to the duck. The *Bell's* hawsers were cast off and Curly, watching his chance, turned the duck around in the lee of the *Bell* and headed for the distant beach.

The first part of the trip was uneventful. The tide,

which had been almost at the ebb when Curly launched the duck, had turned and was running in to shore, helping the amphibian along. The sea had moderated slightly although a heavy ground swell was running and the duck pitched and rolled badly, making it difficult to keep a straight course. They were about a mile from the beach when Holman called to Curly.

"Boat coming up on the port bow," he reported. "It's the Chicamacomico boat."

Curly stood up and stared. A mile away a thirty-eight foot motor boat was plowing through the waves toward them, the high wave rising from her bow giving evidence of the fact that she was being pushed to her top speed.

"I wonder what's eating on Loman?" Curly mused. "He's sure making knots with that old scow."

He held steadily on his way and the beach in front of the old Cape Hatteras lighthouse came steadily nearer. He was still more than a half mile off shore when the Chicamacomico boat crossed his stern, swung around and came alongside, a boat's length from him. Loman Migert was standing in the bow.

"How are you making out, Graham?" he hailed.

"Doing fine, Mr. Migert. How come you got here?"

"Merle phoned Chicamacomico when you started. I was on my way to Little Kinnakeet, so he talked with me on the radio and asked me to come out and look after you. Throw me a line and I'll take you in tow."

"We don't need a tow, Mr. Migert, we're moving right along."

"That you are, but your passenger ought to be got to the hospital as soon as may be. We can't transfer him in this sea."

"No, sir, but he'll be all right here. We've got him lashed to the litter and we're keeping him fairly steady."

"That's true, but I can tow you to Hatteras village much quicker than you can make it under your own power. That's what I'm thinking of."

"I'm going straight in to the plane, Mr. Migert."

"Can you get across the bar in that craft with low water in a sea like this?"

"Yes, sir, I think so. I took her out across the bar at Cape Hatteras with the surf much higher and at almost slack water. I'll have maybe half a fathom more under me coming in than I had going out."

Loman Migert hesitated.

"I'm not going to interfere with a man in command of his own craft," he said. "Your Chief asked me to help you. I'll do whatever you say, but I'll issue no orders. You're responsible for your own command and you'll have to decide."

"I'm going straight in, Mr. Migert."

"Good luck, Graham. You'll probably need it. I'll stand by, of course, but remember, once you get over the bar, I can't help you. I draw too much water to try to go in, across it."

Curly considered the problem for a moment.

"Toss me a heaving line, sir, and I'll send out a hawser. Take a turn around your towing bitt and hold me steady as I reach the bar. I may want to lay by for a minute or two and you can help keep me from broaching."

"Right. Stand by for a line."

A heaving line shot out and Holman caught it. A moment later he bent it to the spliced eye of a short hawser which Loman Migert hauled aboard.

"Be ready to cast off the instant I signal, sir," Curly called.

"Right. I'll handle it myself."

The duck plowed on, the motor boat with her propeller almost idling, following at the length of the hawser. The bar was only a few feet away when Curly slowed his motor and signalled Migert to take up a strain on the hawser and hold him steady. He eyed the tossing water over the bar and for a moment the wisdom of the course he was pursuing

The Duck Goes Out

seemed doubtful. Perhaps it would be best to take a tow to Avon, or to Hatteras.

Suddenly the water in front of him calmed. He blew a sharp blast on his horn and the end of the hawser flew in the air as Loman Migert cast it loose. The motor of the duck roared and the amphibian plunged ahead.

For the first few feet over the bar the water was miraculously smooth and then a huge wave came boiling in. It met a receding wave and the two crashed, tossing spray high in the air. The duck was caught in the turbulent churning and tossed about like a chip. There was a thud as she grounded, then she was high up again in the air, tossed almost out of the water. She came down with a crash, the port gunwale going almost under. A huge wave broke over the stern, pouring gallons of water aboard. The bilge pumps started to send out steady streams, but Curly knew that they could not keep up with many such breakers.

Another cross wave caught the amphibian and for a moment threatened to turn her around and broach her. Curly gunned the motor to the limit and fought desperately with the kicking wheel. Gradually the duck came around and resumed her forward motion toward the shore, but in the turmoil she was tossed wildly about, rolling, pitching and weaving with a corkscrew motion that threatened to toss Curly from the wheel.

Foot by foot the amphibian won her way forward. Now the inner edge of the bar was at hand. The duck shivered as another wave struck, then with a sudden spurt she was over the bar and riding in steadier water. Curly relaxed for an instant. Now there was only one more bad bit, the beach itself and it could not be as bad as the bar had been.

It seemed only a matter of seconds until he was at the edge of the breaking surf. One wave after another smote the duck, breaking over her stern and tossing gallons of water aboard, but there were no cross waves and so long as he could hold her on a straight course and keep her from broaching to, Curly was certain that he could make a landing.

A wave raised the duck and carried her forward on its crest. As the wave broke there was a bone-shaking jar as the wheels of the amphibian struck the sand. Curly threw in his clutch, but a moment later the motor was racing as the wheels spun in the water. Again a wave raised the vehicle and almost turned it sideways. Curly wrenched at the wheel and there was another jar. The wheels spun for an instant, then they gripped and when the next wave raised the amphibian to where the wheels lost contact with the sand, she was three or four lengths nearer her goal.

The Duck Goes Out

The wave passed by and once more the front wheels bit the sand. The duck surged forward and there was a grating sound underneath as the rear wheels caught. They spun aimlessly for a moment, then they gripped and before the next wave could reach and raise her, the duck was churning through shallow water and up onto the dry beach. The landing had been made.

Curly stopped the duck alongside the waiting plane. The pilot of the Goose jumped on the footboard of the duck and extended his hand.

"Fine work, fellow!" he exclaimed heartily. "That was the nicest bit of surf work I've ever seen."

"Thank you, sir," Curly said as a flush mantled his cheek.

"Thank me, nothing, I'm glad to have seen it. Now, we'll take your passenger off your hands and we'll have him in the Marine Hospital in an hour."

The plane crew, aided by Ballard and the cook, lifted the litter down and unfastened the life preservers from it. Carefully they carried it to the plane, whose motors were already turning over, and loaded it aboard. The pilot climbed in with a final wave of his hand. The plane motors roared and the Goose moved off along the beach. It bumped once, then was airborne. It climbed, made a circle around the old lighthouse, then, with a dip of its wings in greeting, it leveled off and headed for Norfolk.

Curly lowered his gaze from the sky and found himself looking into the deepset eyes of Merle Becker. Behind the Chief stood Jeff Davis MacAlpin, a dry smile on his deeply lined face.

"Do you know what an order is, Graham?"

Curly's heart sank.

"Yes, sir, it's something to be obeyed."

"That's what the books say," Becker's deep voice rumbled, "but maybe they don't say enough. Could be an order is something to be disobeyed when it isn't a good order. I don't know, so I won't argue the point. The only orders I ever gave you were to take the duck out and bring the casualty in. You obeyed those orders. Do you understand?"

Curly gasped.

"Yes, sir," he said. "Yes, Chief, I—I understand."

"That remark, Merle, was the quintessence of wisdom," came MacAlpin's dry voice. "By it, credit redounds to you both and harmony reigns. Solomon with all his wisdom, could have done no better."

Curly started to speak, but he was interrupted by a low howl of anguish and utter misery from the duck.

"Surfman!" he gasped as he jumped for the side of the vehicle. "What's the matter?"

The big Chesapeake lay on the floor of the cab, his legs twitching and his jaws open with saliva dribbling from his mouth. In a moment Curly was inside the cab and was lifting the dog in his arms.

"He's sick!" he cried.

Willing hands took the Chesapeake from his arms and laid him gently on the sand. Whimpers of misery came from Surfman. MacAlpin bent down and felt him over with gentle, expert hands. Inch by inch he covered the dog's anatomy and a queer expression came over his face.

"Stand him up, Morgan, get him on feet. Go ahead, I know what I'm doing."

Curly carefully lifted the dog until he stood on uncertain feet, his legs threatening momentarily to buckle under him.

"Now go ahead and call to him to follow."

Hesitantly, Curly took a step forward.

"Come, Surfman," he said.

The dog tried to follow, but he swayed and staggered as though he were about to collapse utterly. He went ahead for a few steps, then he lowered his head. A moment later, MacAlpin burst into laughter.

"He'll feel lots better now he's rid of that," he chuckled. "There's just one thing the matter with him, Morgan, he's badly seasick. In fact, I doubt if I've ever seen a much more acute attack."

"Seasick!" Curly cried in amazement.

"Yes, and after that trip across the bar, I think

it's a fully justified case. I almost lost my lunch just watching that duck hop around."

"Seasick!" Curly's voice held half reproach, half amusement. "You, Surfman, getting seasick like a landsman at boot camp. I ought to change your name to Seaman Apprentice. What's the thing to do for him, Mr. MacAlpin?"

"Oh, just walk him around for a bit. He'll live, although right now he probably hopes he won't."

"I'll walk him all right," Curly said with a grin. "Jake, drive the duck up to the station, will you? I'll be up in a few minutes and we'll hose her down with fresh water and secure her. Wait a minute. Chief, would you rather I'd help with the duck or work on the surfboat motor tonight?"

"Work on the duck," Becker answered in his slow, rumbling voice. "I can use a surfboat, but from the way you handled that duck today, I think, of the two, I'd rather have it ready for action."

"Yes, sir. Okay, Jake, take her away. I'm going to walk this silly dog home and see if he can't get his land legs again. Come on, Surfman, get up. Surfman, *come!*"

With a colossal sigh, Surfman struggled to his feet. With hanging head and drooping tail, he followed his master, swaying from side to side as he walked and stopping at intervals to lower his head and gag.

"It *was* a rough trip, Surfman," Curly said, "but, as Mr. MacAlpin says, you'll live. Come on."

Whimpering in self pity and looking as though he were certain he had not a friend on earth, the big Chesapeake lurched along with lowered head at his master's heels.

The Damficare

"Now what?" Chief Becker grumbled as he lifted the telephone receiver from its hook. "Cape Hatteras Life Boat Station, Becker speaking."

"Chief, this is Herb Scarsdale, in the tower. Could you come up here for a minute?"

"What's the matter?"

"There's a boat out there that acts like she's in trouble."

"What sort of trouble?"

"Could be a jammed tiller or a broken tiller cable, sir. A little while ago she was running around in crazy circles. Right now she's drifting in with the tide. She'll be on the bar in another half hour, looks like."

"Is she flying a distress signal?"

"No, sir."

"Well, I'll come up and take a look at her."

Becker puffed his way up the tower and took the

The Damficare

binoculars which Scarsdale handed to him. Two miles south, just off the point of Cape Hatteras, a cabin cruiser bobbed lazily about on the light swell.

"I can't see anybody aboard," he said as he stared through the glasses. "She isn't anchored, is she?"

"No, sir, she's drifting. A while ago I thought I could see a man at the wheel—that was when she was running fast—but I can't see anyone aboard now."

Becker's gaze swept the ocean, searching for a small boat in which the cruiser's crew could have left her, but, aside from the cruiser herself, the sea was empty. Not even a fishing boat was in sight. He turned the glasses again on the cruiser but her appearance had not changed since his first scrutiny.

"Looks like she's abandoned," he rumbled in his deep voice. "I'd better send someone out to have a look at her. "Only trouble is, I haven't anyone to send. Keep an eye on her, Herb, and let me know if there's any change or if you see anyone aboard."

He climbed down the tower, mentally calling the roll of the station and wondering where he could dig up a boat crew to send out. The motor boat was out with two men inspecting the Hatteras Inlet navigation aids, one man was at the Loran tower, one was recharging the batteries of the light, one was sick, two were on liberty, one was on tower watch—

"Nobody here but me and the cook," he grumbled. "How they ever expect me to run a station like this with a crew of eleven men is beyond me. I'll have to call Wyman and Corey back from the light and the Loran. Hooky can relieve Herb on the tower and I reckon the four of us can launch the motor surfboat if we have to. No use sending the dory out because it looks like a tow job. Well—Oh, hello, Surfman, where did you come from?"

The Chesapeake wagged his tail in reply but continued on his way. Curly, dressed in a greasy suit of denims, came around the corner of the station, whistling gaily. Becker stared at him.

"I thought you were on liberty," he said.

"I am, Chief, but I decided not to go to Manteo with Jake this morning. Instead, I stayed here and greased the duck. I'm going fishing with Old Joey after dinner."

A sudden light came into Becker's face.

"Is the duck all right?" he asked.

"Couldn't be better, Chief."

"Could you take her out alone? There's no surf to speak of."

"I can take her out alone any time, surf or no surf. Where do you want me to go?"

"Wel-l-l, I hate to recall your liberty, but there's a cabin cruiser off shore that acts like something was wrong and we can't see anyone aboard her. I was

The Damficare

about to call in everyone and try to scratch up a crew to send the motor surfboat out, but if you—"

"Chief, I'm practically on my way. Where is this derelict?"

"Off the point of the Cape, a little north of it, and drifting toward the bar. If you can get a line to her before she grounds, it'll be a lot easier than dragging her off later after she's settled in the sand."

"What shall I do with her after I get her?"

"Use your judgment. If there's anyone aboard, give them what help you can. If not, about the only thing to do is to tow her to Hatteras. If you start towing, I'll radio the motor boat to come out through the Inlet to meet you and take her off your hands."

"Okay, Chief, I'll get a towing hawser and be on my way in a couple of minutes."

"Thanks, Curly, I'll make up the lost liberty to you."

"Forget it, Chief, I'd just as soon make a cruise in the duck as to go fishing; rather, in fact. Say, would you mind phoning Little Kinnakeet and ask them to get word to Old Joey that I'm tied up and can't go out with him today?"

"That I'll do, Curly."

The worried expression left Becker's face as Curly went to the stores locker and came back with a coil of heavy rope looped over his shoulder. He tossed the coil into the duck, then turned and spoke with mock sternness to the expectant Surfman, who was eagerly awaiting his master's command to leap into the amphibian.

"You can't go, you clumsy landlubber," he said. "You'd get seasick and I'm not going to mop up after you again. You stay ashore."

The Chesapeake's head fell and his tail drooped disconsolately at his master's words. He stared up at Curly, but the man's expression did not change and Surfman's tail drooped another notch until it was almost between his legs. With a crushed air, he turned around and stared slowly toward the station. Curly burst into laughter.

"Okay, fellow, I couldn't do you that much dirt. Come aboard. But remember one thing, you've got to redeem yourself this trip or next time I *will* leave you ashore."

Surfman's head went up and his tail swung in a vigorous arc. With a long, graceful leap he rose in the air and his front paws caught over the edge of the duck's cab, A sharp scramble and he was in the vehicle, his tail pounding vigorously and his eyes alert. Curly patted his head for a moment, then pressed the starter button and the motor of the amphibian woke to noisy life. A few minutes later the duck was on the beach near the point of Cape Hatteras, her nose to sea, while Curly studied the surf and waited for the opportune moment to launch her.

He did not have to wait long. The tide was coming in, but the surf was light and there was no ground swell to complicate his task. A wave broke on the beach and started to run back out to sea. The duck followed the line of the retreating water until the wheels were awash. Another wave came in and the amphibian lurched forward. The front wheels raised off the sand and then the vehicle was waterborne and her propeller bit the water, sending her forward into the gently surging water.

"Not much like the last time, is it, Surfman?" Curly chuckled, "I expect even a landsman like you are can keep his dinner down today."

The Chesapeake thumped his tail in reply, his gaze fixed on the water ahead of the duck, which was plowing steadily forward at six knots. With no ground swell to speak of and with the tide half in, Curly knew there would be plenty of water over the bar and he did not even slow the vehicle down as they approached. The cabin cruiser was within two hundred yards of the outer edge of the bar and the tide was carrying it steadily shoreward.

"*Ahoy!*" Curly hailed as he approached the drifting boat, on whose stern was emblazoned the name "*DAMFICARE*" and the port "NEW YORK." "*Ahoy!* Aboard the *Damficare!*"

There was no reply to his hail and he swung the duck around, circling close to the drifting boat. It was, to all appearance, abandoned, and his repeated hails brought no response.

"I reckon we'll have to tow it," he remarked to Surfman who was staring intently at the boat and who had reinforced his master's hail with vigorous barking. "Here is where I wish I had a crew. Oh, yes, I know you'll help, but you can't handle a boat hook or pass a line."

He dropped rope bumpers over the side of the duck to protect the paint, then laid a boat hook and lashing lines ready before he returned to the cab and restarted his motor. He swung about in a wide circle, then directed his course so that he would run up to the port side of the cruiser. When he was within a few yards, he killed his motor and scrambled out of the cab and stood on the deck, boat hook in hand.

The gap between the two boats narrowed slowly. Curly reached with the boat hook and caught the cruiser's gunwale and pulled steadily. As they touched he dropped the hook and lashed them firmly together fore and aft, then, with Surfman at his heels, he jumped aboard the derelict. As he did so he felt a slight bump, then a grating sound from the hull of the *Damficare*. Already they were on the outer edge of the bar and the incoming tide would

The Damficare

soon drive them onto the clinging sand unless he worked rapidly.

The duck, seaworthy as she was, had little pulling power and Curly did not relish the task of trying to haul the larger boat off the sand, once she was firmly lodged. He jumped back into the amphibian and restarted the silent motor. With a prayer that the light lashings which bound them together would hold under the strain, he cramped his rudder hard to port and gradually speeded up his motor.

The keel of the cruiser grated and ground against the bottom and for a few minutes it was nip and tuck as the propeller of the duck churned the water into foam. Gradually the steady pull of the amphibian's motor won over the force of the tide and inch by inch the two boats slid forward. Now the effects of the duck's rudder began to make itself felt and slowly and ponderously the lashed boats turned about and moved out toward the open sea. The lashings held and Curly drove steadily ahead until the boats were three hundred yards from the bar. There he once more stopped his motor and jumped aboard the *Damficare* to learn, if he could, what had put her in the predicament in which he had found her.

The wheel house offered no clue. The boat's ignition had been cut off, but a glance at the fuel gauge showed Curly that the tanks were more than half full. The wheel was not lashed, but when he tested it, it handled normally. Evidently the steering cables were intact and the rudder was not jammed. On the forward deck an anchor was properly lashed in place. There was nothing to indicate that anything had happened to force the abandonment of the boat. The floor of the wheel house was littered with cigarette butts and burned matches and in one corner lay a pile of broken glass, evidently the remains of a smashed tumbler. Puzzled, Curly left the wheel house and went aft to the well deck.

Here the boat gave the impression of having been hastily abandoned. A fishing rod, rigged and with the line trailing over the side into the water, stood in the starboard rod socket. The port socket was empty, but another rod lay on the deck as though some one had dropped it hastily without even taking time to put it in the socket or to lean it against the gunwale. The floor of the well deck, like the wheel house, was littered with cigarette butts and burned matches.

"What do you make of it, Surfman?" Curly asked.

The Chesapeake, who had been sniffing inquiringly at the various items, looked up at his master and wagged his tail tentatively.

"Got you licked too, has it? Well, I reckon as how the only thing for us to do is to take her in tow and head for Hatteras. Hello, what's that?"

Surfman swung around, his ears pricked forward,

The Damficare

and stared at the door of the cabin. As Curly followed the direction of the dog's gaze, a thin trickle of sound came from the cabin, a sound which made prickles run up and down his spine. It was a weird, unearthly sound, a mixture of a moan and a whine. There was a moment of silence and then the sound came again, this time mingled with a gurgle that made Curly instinctively think of blood bubbling from a slashed throat. The sound died away, then it came again, this time distinctly a moan. Curly gripped hard on the gunwale, his face bedewed with sweat.

Surfman started slowly forward toward the cabin and Curly, fighting down a rising tide of panic, followed the dog. The sound came again and Curly let out his breath in a long gasp. Courage and calmness surged back into him and he stepped resolutely through the hatchway into the dark interior of the cabin. For a moment he could see nothing and his hand sought for a light switch. He could not find one, but in a few moments his eyes became accustomed to the gloom and he groped his way to one of the bunks before which Surfman was standing.

On the bunk was a sprawled figure. As his eyes grew more accustomed to the gloom, Curly could see that it was a man. He lay sprawled out on the bunk, fully clothed. His jaw hung open and from his lips came the eerie sounds that had frightened the Coastguardsman. Curly quickly bent over the man, his fingers automatically searching for his pulse. It was beating strongly and regularly, nor could Curly find any signs of a blow on the head or any other injury that would account for his condition.

A half-choked grunt came from behind him and Curly whirled about. On the opposite bunk sprawled another man, this one attired only in a pair of bathing trunks and soft shoes. Suddenly Curly was aware that the cabin was filled with fumes of some sort, fumes which made him momentarily choke.

"Gas fumes!" he exclaimed. "Both of them overcome!"

He bent over the man wearing the trunks and strove to lift him up to carry him from the fume-laden cabin into the open air. As he raised the victim he saw that the man held something firmly gripped in his hand. Curly's eyes had become accustomed to the gloom by now and the identity of the object the unconscious man was hanging on to with a death grip was painfully evident. It was a half-empty bottle, the label of which proclaimed its contents to be whisky.

"Well, I'll be darned!" Curly exclaimed in disgust.

He bent forward and sniffed at the man's breath. There was no question as to the malady from which he was suffering. He was simply drunk. His companion, as Curly quickly learned by investigation, was in the same condition. He straightened up and surveyed the two prone figures, wrath fighting with disgust on his face.

"Bite them, Surfman," he said grimly. "No, don't, they'd probably poison you if you did. I'll tow them into Hatteras all right. I've got to, but I'd a lot rather tow them into jail."

With Surfman following him, he strode back to the well deck and jumped aboard the duck. He was back in a few minutes with a coil of hawser and tossed the spliced eye over a cleat on the forward deck of the *Damficare,* a name which suddenly had meaning to him.

"No, I expect they don't," he grunted. "They don't care what happens to them or to somebody they might run into, or to some poor Coast Guard who might have to risk his life in a storm to get them ashore."

He fastened the other end of the hawser to the duck's towing bitt, then returned to the cruiser. First one and then the other of the two men he hauled out of the cabin into the well deck, then picked up a bucket with a line bent to the bail. He lowered the bucket over the side and when he hauled it up full of seawater, it was a feeling of sardonic satisfaction that he sluiced the contents over the prone figures. Both of them spluttered and when Curly had doused them with a second bucket of water, the one wearing bathing trunks struggled to a sitting position.

"Hey, whazza idea?" he spluttered. "Whazzsher doin?"

He strove to rise and Curly caught him by the hand and heaved him up, only to have him collapse into a chair.

"Whazza idea?" he demanded again. "Whazzsher tryin do?"

"Are you the owner of this boat?" Curly demanded.

"Shure I am. Wanner make something out of it?" the man demanded truculently.

"I'm Machinist's Mate Graham of the Coast Guard," Curly said, slowly and clearly. "You are in no condition to navigate and I'm taking charge here. I'm towing your boat back to Hatteras. Do you understand?"

"Shure, I unnerstand. You're stealing my boat, my lovely, beautiful boat. Only boat I got."

He looked around and maudlin tears ran down his fat face. Curly looked at him in disgust.

"I'm towing your boat to Hatteras," he repeated slowly and distinctly. "Try to sober up enough to disembark when we get there. You'd better try to sober your partner up too. Come on, Surfman, let's get off this floating saloon before we get a few more whiffs of those breaths and get pie-eyed ourselves."

Followed by the Chesapeake, he jumped aboard the duck, which by this time had drifted perilously close once more to the edge of the bar. Curly quickly threw off the lashing which held the boats side by side, then took in the towing hawser until the bow of the *Damficare* would ride only a few yards behind the duck's stern. When he had the tow adjusted to his satisfaction, he started the amphibian's motor and set his course for the long tow to Hatteras. Surfman, his eyes alternately looking ahead at the empty sea and back at the cruiser bobbing along in their wake, sat in the cab beside him.

Surfman Redeems Himself

THE DUCK, with the *Damficare* in tow, plowed steadily along through the calm sea. The amphibian wallowed as the waves broke against her port side but the motion was so slight as to be soothing rather than distressing. They were making, as nearly as Curly could estimate, about four knots. At that rate, it would take them many hours to reach Hatteras but Curly proceeded at normal cruising speed and made no attempt to push the duck to the limit. Becker had promised to radio the motor boat and it was probably already on its way to meet them and take over the tow so that the duck could return to the station.

"Now, if we had just stolen one of those rods we saw, Surfman," Curly said to the dog who sat beside him, "we could fish on the way in. I hope Old Joey isn't too disappointed; he's been after me to go fishing with him for the last two weeks. Oh, well, there are lots more days coming."

He stood up and looked around. There was not a boat in sight except a tanker on the extreme horizon, beating her way south. Curly dropped back into the seat and resigned himself to the monotonous job of towing. Surfman curled up and dropped his head on his paws. Curly yawned vociferously and, lulled by the heat of the sun and the gentle rocking of the duck, allowed himself to relapse into a daydream, his thoughts many miles from Hatteras Island.

Aboard the *Damficare* the two men whom Curly had hauled from the cabin lay sprawled out on chairs. The momentarily reviving effect of the seawater with which he had doused them had passed and they had relapsed into drunken slumber. Presently the man in trunks stirred uneasily. He squirmed about uncomfortably in his chair and gave an uneasy, convulsive jerk. It disturbed his balance and he crashed to the deck. At the shock of his fall, he opened his eyes and stared vacantly around, then shook his head violently and rubbed his face. Gradually traces of remembrance began to trickle into his befuddled brain. He sat erect suddenly.

"Kidnapped!" he gasped. "Boat stolen. Pirates. Where's Slug?"

His wandering gaze spied his companion slumped in a chair. He rose to unsteady feet and crossed the deck.

"Hey, Slug!" he said, shaking the prone figure. "Wake up. Slug!"

The other man stirred uneasily and shook his head.

"Lemme sleep," he mumbled. "G'way. Lemme sleep."

"Wake up, Slug, we're kidnapped. Wake up, you drunken bum. What do you think I hire you for, to sleep all day?"

He shook his companion vigorously. Slug's eyes opened. He blinked in the bright sunlight and stared around with a befuddled gaze. Slowly his eyes began to focus and he rose from the chair.

"We're moving," he announced. He balanced himself on unsteady legs and looked around. "We're being towed," he declared with an air of triumph at having solved the mystery. "Towed by a blooming truck. Where did you get tow, Mr. Crogan?"

"Pirates," Crogan declared solemnly. "Pirates kidnapped us. Taking us to desert island. Make us walk plank."

Slug pondered over his employer's statement.

"No pirates," he said, shaking his head with an owlish stare. "No pirates. Pirates all gone long ago."

"It's pirates," Crogan insisted. "Stole my boat. Only pirates steal boats. You know that."

"Okay, you're boss," Slug agreed. "What you wanna do about it?"

"Recapture boats. Kill bloody pirates. Hang 'em to yardarm."

"Can't. No yardarm."

"What happened to it?"

"Boat never had yardarm."

"I was cheated. Man said boat had everything. Bloody liar. No yardarm."

"Don't need yardarm."

"How we gonna hang pirates without yardarm?"

"Make 'em walk plank."

"We gotta plank?"

"Make them furnish plank."

"Sure, thass good idea. Let's get going."

"What we gonna do?"

"First we'll escape. Then we'll capture plank and make 'em walk pirates."

"Can't escape," Slug remonstrated. "Truck's towing us."

"Sure we can. Truck can't float on water, Cut truck loose and it'll sink. Let's cut truck loose and sink pirates. Save trouble hanging them."

"Thassa good idea, Mr. Crogan. I'll get axe."

Slug staggered to the after bulkhead and took a fireaxe from its rack.

"Wait a minute," Crogan said. "They might board us. Must repel boarders. I'll get cutlasses and muskets."

He disappeared into the cabin and returned with two kitchen knives, an automatic pistol and a high-powered sporting rifle.

"Prepare to repel boarders!" he said, offering the weapons to his companion. Slug thrust one of the butcher knives under his belt and after vainly trying to do the same with the pistol, he stuffed it into his pocket. Crogan tried to emulate his companion but after cutting himself in his attempt to get the knife under the elastic band of his trunks, he gripped it in his teeth. Holding the rifle in one hand, he picked up the fireaxe with the other.

"You start motor, Slug. I'll cut truck loose and sink bloody pirates."

"Thassa idea," Slug said approvingly. "I'll start bloody motor."

They staggered forward on uncertain feet. At the wheel house Slug stumbled and half fell inside but Crogan continued on his way until he was at the cleat on the forward deck to which Curly had fastened the towing hawser. He dropped the rifle and took the fireaxe in both hands. Balancing himself on unsteady feet, he raised the axe high overhead and swung it down with his full strength.

He missed the hawser and the keen blade bit

deep into the polished deck. Crogan looked at it in surprise, then wrenched it loose and poised himself for another blow. The twin motors of the *Damficare* turned over, caught, choked, caught again and then roared into life. Crogan swung the axe and this time he struck the hawser. The severed ends flew up and the two craft floated clear. Slug engaged his clutch and the *Damficare* shot forward under the impetus of her twin motors. A moment later there was a sickening thud as her bow struck the duck's stern a glancing blow. The two boats ground together for a moment, then the *Damficare* sheered off and passed by, leaving the amphibian rocking perilously in her wake.

"Thassa stuff, Slug!" Crogan cried as he got to his hands and knees. "Sink old truck. Drown the bloody pirates!"

Slug spun the wheel. The *Damficare* swung around in a wide circle and then came charging back toward the amphibian, a growing wave coming from her sharp bow as she picked up speed.

Curly's first intimation of what was going on aboard the cruiser came when Crogan's blow severed the hawser. Relieved of the weight of the tow, the duck lurched suddenly forward, almost burying her nose in the water. Surfman slid off the seat on which he had been curled up and Curly was thrown back hard against the seat cushion. Before he could recall his wandering thoughts and realize what had happened, the duck lurched again as the *Damficare* rammed her on the stern. The cruiser grated forward and the duck heeled over until she began to ship water. Curly wrenched at the rudder but there was nothing he could do. For a moment the issue hung in doubt, then the pressure was relieved as the cruiser sheered off and the amphibian righted herself with a wallow.

"What the devil!" Curly cried as he jumped to his feet and looked around. "What happened?"

A few yards away the *Damficare*, with both motors roaring, was driving ahead. As he watched the cruiser swung around and headed directly toward him.

"*Hey!*" Curly shouted. "*Look out!* SHEER OFF!"

The cruiser came steadily ahead and Curly suddenly realized that her actions were deliberate. It was the evident intention of the *Damficare's* pilot to ram the amphibian amidships. The thin steel walls of the duck would not withstand a blow like that. Even if she were not overturned, the blow would punch a gaping hole in her side and the amphibian would sink like a lead plummet. There was only one chance and that was a slim one. Curly gunned his motor, coaxing from the duck every particle of speed that he could. He ground his wheel hard to starboard, striving to make the amphibian's course parallel that of her assailant. If he could turn the duck enough so that the *Damficare's* sharp prow would strike only a glancing blow, there was a chance that the amphibian would escape serious injury.

The duck's head came around slowly. The cruiser was coming fast and Curly's face was white and grim as he calculated the chances. If he turned too far and there were a head-on collision the result might be worse than if he allowed himself to be rammed amidships, for the *Damficare's* bow might be stove in and both vessels go to the bottom. If he could be sure that the cruiser would hold on a straight course, he could calculate with some certainty of success, but Slug was swaying at the wheel and with each sway, the *Damficare's* course altered.

It was over in a moment. The *Damficare* charged ahead, Crogan on the front deck brandishing the rifle and bellowing obscenities. When the two vessels were only a few lengths apart, Slug slipped and fell sideways. He dragged the wheel with him and the cruiser made a sudden swerve. For an instant it seemed possible that she would cross the duck's wake without striking her, then there was a crash which sent the duck sideways with enough tip that water slopped over her bow. Crogan fell sprawling on the cruiser's deck. The rifle went off with a crash and a round hole appeared in the amphibian's windshield in front of Curly's eyes. The bullet had missed him by inches.

Slug recovered his footing and spun the *Damficare's* wheel.

"Thassa stuff, Slug, old boy, old boy," Crogan chortled as he sat up on the deck. "Sink bloody pirates. I'll repel boarders."

The crash of the heavy sporting rifle had been music in his ears. He had found a new toy to play with and as quickly as his fumbling hands could work the bolt, he fired in the general direction of the duck.

Once more the cruiser made a wide circle and was approaching the duck at top speed.

"This can't go on," Curly cried desperately. "Sooner or later, he'll hit us square and then . . ."

He would have to board the cruiser some way. He snatched a life preserver from its hook and shrugged it on. There was no time to fasten it, but he could take care of that detail later. The *Damficare* was coming fast and Curly wrenched his wheel desperately to put the duck at a quartering angle to the cruiser's course. The clumsy amphibian responded sluggishly to her rudder, but she came slowly around. Curly remained at the wheel until the two vessels were only two lengths apart, then he left the cab, Surfman at his heels and poised himself on the deck of the duck, his muscles tensed for a leap.

The sharp prow of the cruiser split the water, holding a steady course. The duck was still turning sluggishly, but it was evident that the blow was going to be a more severe one than either of the former. Curly poised on the balls of his feet, moving along the deck toward the point where the sharp bow would strike. A fraction of a second before the crash, he sprang.

The cruiser's bow towered over the low deck of the duck. Curly leaped high in the air and his chest struck the gunwale of the *Damficare*. The two vessels came together with a grinding crash and Curly gave a cry of pain as his dangling legs were caught between them. For a moment the pressure increased, then it eased off and Curly struggled desperately to reach the cruiser's deck. There was a deafening crash as the rifle went off in his face and he could hear the crack of the bullet past his ear. He clawed at the polished deck but he seemed to win his way upward at an agonizingly slow rate. His legs refused to obey his orders. He tried to bring them up, but they dangled helplessly and his hands could gain no hold on the smooth boards.

· Crogan had again been thrown sprawling by the shock of the collision, but he was scrambling to a sitting position, the rifle still gripped in his hands.

"Repel boarders!" he shouted happily as his hands fumbled with the bolt of the rifle. An empty cartridge case tinkled on the deck and the bolt closed with a snap. Crogan raised the rifle to his shoulder and the muzzle wavered in an uncertain circle. Gradually its orbit decreased in size and Curly found himself staring down the barrel of the weapon. He stared in fascination at the hole from which the bullet would come, unable to move a muscle. From the corner of his eye he could see Crogan's fingers fumbling for the trigger. Suddenly they found it and for Curly time ceased to exist. It seemed that he stared for hours, for days, at the gun muzzle, waiting for the flash, the roar, the crash of the bullet which would spell oblivion. He wanted to scream, to cry out to his adversary to pull the trigger, to end the suspense, but his throat had so contracted that he could not force a sound past his lips. Involuntarily his eyes closed and he waited—waited—waited—

There was a blinding flash, visible even through his closed eyelids, a shattering roar in his ears, and then a scream of pain. Curly's eyes flashed open. The rifle lay on the deck and Crogan was bellowing in mingled rage and fear as he strove to fight off the mahogany mass of canine rage that was earnestly driving for the erstwhile gunner's throat.

Suddenly Curly was master of himself again.

"No, Surfman, *no!*" he cried. "*Down sir,* DOWN!"

Obedient, even in his rage, the big Chesapeake dropped to a crouch, but his lips were drawn back in a vicious snarl and his eyes were fixed balefully on his opponent. As Crogan threw out his hand and strove to rise, Surfman lunged forward, his teeth bared.

"*Down, Surfman!*" Curly cried again. "Lie still, you ass," he barked at Crogan. "If you reach for that gun again, I won't be able to control him. *Lie still,* I tell you!"

Crogan ceased his movement and Surfman dropped again to a crouch, but his eye did not for an instant leave the prone man.

Curly clawed at the deck and found that his legs would once more move as he directed them. They seemed curiously numb and unresponsive, but he could move them with difficulty and he managed to scramble up onto the deck beside Crogan.

"I'll take charge of this," he said as he grasped the rifle. "Lie still, I tell you," he snapped at Crogan who was again trying to rise, an attempt which made Surfman edge closer and crouch lower for a spring.

"Steady, Surfman," Curly said warningly. "Good dog, you got here just in time. Good boy. I wonder how you got aboard."

The Chesapeake sank back once more but he did not abate his alertness, although his tail pounded the deck vigorously at his master's praise. He had been poised alongside his master as the cruiser approached. The shock of the collision had thrown him momentarily off balance, but he got quickly to his feet and, as the *Damficare* started to veer away, he had made a mighty spring through the air. The cruiser was almost beyond reach, but his front paws caught the gunwale amidships and he hung on, clawing and fighting to gain the deck. For a moment it was nip and tuck, but the dog had had much experience in climbing aboard boats and gradually his efforts were effective. He scrambled over the rail and raced forward toward the spot where he had last seen his master. As he mounted the front deck he had paused for an instant, then the meaning of the tableau before him became clear. With a mighty roar of rage he had launched his sturdy body through the air and his powerful teeth slashed into Crogan's bare flank just as his fingers closed on the rifle's trigger. The gun flew from Crogan's grip and Surfman sprang for his adversary's throat. Had Curly's command come a moment later it would have been useless, for Surfman's attack was already launched. He had time merely to snap his teeth shut before his hard muzzle had struck Crogan and sprawled him flat on the deck.

Curly drew up his legs and fingered them experimentally. They were numb and unfeeling, but he could move them as he wished. He was fairly sure they would support him and he got them under him with an effort. Slowly he rose and stood swaying. A moment later stabs and flashes of pain ran down his legs, centering in his left knee. He tried to walk, but his left leg gave way and he crumpled to the deck, the stabs of pain coming more rapidly and with greater intensity. He bit his lips to keep from screaming. Crogan, on the deck beside him, was blubbering and rubbing at his lacerated side. The *Damficare*, with no one at the wheel, was charging ahead aimlessly across the water.

When Slug had staggered into the wheel house in obedience to his employer's orders, his head was spinning from the liquor he had consumed. The brief sleep he had had was not enough to clear his brain from the fumes of whisky, but it had been long enough to give him an overwhelming thirst for more. As he bent over the ignition switch to start the motors, he spied a partly full bottle on the map shelf beside him. With an exclamation of satisfaction he put the bottle to his lips and let the fiery liquid run down his throat. In a few minutes conscious or coherent thought became impossible to him and his subsequent actions in striving to ram the duck were automatic and not those of a rational being. Later, when he would recover from his stupor, he would have not the faintest remembrance of his actions.

He hung on to the wheel, turning it and guiding the cruiser with a skill based on long experience, yet it was his inability to concentrate on the task and guide his muscles intelligently that was responsible for the amphibian's escape from being rammed amidships and capsized or sunk. He swayed uncertainly on his feet as the fresh liquor he had imbibed began to take effect. For a time he maintained his footing by hanging on to the wheel for support, but the last time the vessels had crashed together he slipped and fell sprawling. He lay prone for a minute, then strove to rise. Once he got as far his knees before he collapsed again to the floor. He lay motionless, striving to muster his strength and to get control of his muscles, but the effort was useless. His head fell sideways and he lapsed into a drunken stupor. Even the crash of Crogan's rifle failed to rouse him.

Curly lay on the deck, sweat pouring out all over him from the agonizing pain of his crushed knee. He tried to grip it, but the touch of his hands increased the pain. Yet, something must be done. There was no one at the wheel of the cruiser and he must some way reach the wheel house and get the boat under control.

"Surfman," he groaned. "If you could only handle a boat!"

The Chesapeake rose and came over, licking at his master's face.

"I know, old fellow, you'll do all you can, you've done that. Lord, if this pain would only let up for an instant!"

He rolled over and got slowly up on his uninjured knee. It was sheer agony, and sweat poured down his face, but inch by inch he levered himself across the heaving deck toward the wheel house, Surfman at his side.

Suddenly the dog bared his teeth and turned back. Crogan had started to rise.

"*Lie still*, I told you!" Curly grated through set teeth. "If you try to move again, I'll set the dog on you, not call him off."

Crogan sunk back and Curly resumed his laborious progress. A foot at a time he made his way forward until he came to the three steps leading up into the wheel house. Here he was stumped. It was impossible for him to lever himself up that elevation with his hands alone and his left leg was useless. He pondered the problem, then a solution came to him.

"Up, Surfman!" he said. "Inside."

With a bark of comprehension the Chesapeake bounded past his master and up into the wheel house. Jumping into a truck or into a boat was a familiar thing to him.

"Here," Curly said, reaching up with one hand. "Come here."

The dog came closer and Curly caught his collar.

"Inside, Surfman!" he commanded. "Get in!"

The dog was puzzled for a moment.

"Good dog," Curly gasped through set teeth as a fresh wave of pain swept over him. "Go ahead. Inside!"

Suddenly Surfman understood. He lunged forward into the wheel house. Curly hung on with one hand while he hauled himself up by the rail with the other. He got partially inside and then Surfman turned back. His strong teeth gripped the shoulder of his master's jacket and he pulled valiantly. Curly gave an involuntary cry of anguish as his injured knee struck the floor, but he hung on and a moment later was sprawling on the wheel house floor.

"There's the other one," he grunted as he saw the prostrate and snoring Slug. "He's out of action, thank goodness."

Slowly and painfully, an inch at a time, he dragged himself across the floor until he could reach the throttle. A moment later the twin motors were idling, giving the *Damficare* merely steerage way.

"Now, if I can just get up!" Curly groaned.

Surfman Redeems Himself

He caught the wheel and hauled himself slowly upright until he was balancing on his right leg. As he looked out, he gave a gasp of relief. Less than a mile away and headed north along the coast, a sturdy motor boat was cutting its way through the waves. At its fore flew the red and white barred ensign of the Coast Guard.

Curly fumbled for a moment before he found the button of the horn, then sent a call for help moaning across the water. The motor boat changed its course and headed toward him. Balancing himself on one leg, Curly spun the wheel and the cruiser swung around to meet the rescuing craft.

In five minutes the motor boat was alongside and Jake Holman was in the wheel house of the *Damficare*.

"Good grief, Curly!" he gasped. "What happened? Are you hurt? Who in thunder is this?"

"Never mind me, I'll tell you later," Curly gasped through white lips. "Find the duck."

"The duck. What are you talking about? Where is it?"

"At sea, running with full throttle. I left it half an hour ago. Find it before it runs out to sea or piles up on the beach."

"Okay." Holman cast a quick glance around the wheel house, then called down to the motor boat. "Barron, come aboard and bring the binocs."

He took the glasses from Migert and mounted to the top of the wheel house.

"I see her," he cried. "She's about four or five miles north and headed up the beach."

"Get her," Curly gasped. "Then take—this—this—"

He swayed for a moment, hanging on to the wheel, then slid to the floor. Migert bent over him with a cry of alarm.

"Jake!" he shouted. "Curly's passed out."

Holman jumped down. He grasped the situation in a moment and orders tumbled from his lips.

"Here, give me a hand, we want to get Curly on that bench."

A moan of pain came from Curly's unconscious lips as the two men lifted him and laid him on the leather covered seat. Surfman crowded close and licked his master's trailing hand. Holman went on.

"Take over the motor boat, Barron," he said. "Radio the Chief and tell him to call Air Rescue and have an ambulance plane flown to Hatteras. Two—no, three—patients. Then go north until you find the duck. She's running free and is four or five miles north. Find her and take her in tow, then call the Chief for orders. I'm taking this boat into Hatteras."

"Okay, Jake."

Migert jumped into the motor boat and its radio

began to buzz. Holman opened the throttles of the cruiser and it slid through the water, swinging around to head to the south.

Suddenly Surfman cocked his head and listened. A deep growl came from his throat and he leaped out of the wheel house and charged forward. Crogan had risen to his knees and was reaching for the rifle which Curly had left on the deck. As the Chesapeake came into sight, his fangs bared and charging down on him, Crogan gave a cry of alarm and dropped quickly to the deck, throwing the rifle from him. Surfman stopped his rush and went forward, a step at a time, with stiff legs, the hackles on his neck raised and his fangs bared, while a murderous growl rumbled in his throat.

"Surfman, come back here!" Holman cried.

The Chesapeake continued his steady, menacing advance. Holman cut the throttle and sprang to the deck, grasping the dog by the collar. He was about to administer a cuff to the dog, but something made him hold his hand.

"I don't know what's been going on here, Surfman," he said, "and you do, so I'd better let you have your way, just so long as you don't actually try to kill this guy. All right, you watch him and don't let him get up, so long as you think that's the proper thing to do. You keep order aboard and I'll dynamite this scow into Hatteras."

He returned to the wheel house and opened the throttles wide. Surfman, with a final warning growl, left the prostrate Crogan and returned to his master's side. He sniffed at Curly, whimpered in sympathy and then began to lick his master's hand.

Missing

THE JEEP drew up in front of the Cape Hatteras Life Boat Station and Jeff Davis MacAlpin uncoiled his long legs and climbed out.

"Merle," he said dryly. "I regret at times that I do not have your weight. If I did, this jet-propelled sand flea might not toss me about as lightly and as nonchalantly as it now does."

"If you did, we'd probably break the springs between us," Becker rumbled as he laboriously extricated himself from the driver's seat. "Well, come on in and wash up. Hooky will have supper ready soon."

"No, I believe I had better go back to my own vine and fig tree. Mike is doubtless yowling around, indignant that his evening repast has been delayed."

"Nonsense, Jeff, you'll stay for supper. Let Mike forage for himself."

"I fear that is what Mike's inclinations run to and I don't wish to encourage him. I beat his ears down regularly to warn him that nesting birds are not a suitable diet for him, but if I fail to provide other sustenance for him regularly, my argument lacks validity."

"We're having chili beans tonight, Jeff, Hooky's specialty."

"You tempt me sorely, Merle."

"And apple pie. Deep dish apple pie—with cheese."

"How the lusts of the flesh do battle with the proddings of conscience," MacAlpin said with a colossal sigh. "I admit that I hunger and that your arguments are almost unanswerable, especially the argument of the pie."

"Well, come on in and if your conscience bothers you—although I never saw any real signs of your having one—I'll send a man up with a meal for Mike."

"Such gracious hospitality overwhelms me, Merle, and renders me helpless. I accept."

He followed Becker up the steps to the station office. Jake Holman, who was sitting at the desk, jumped to his feet as they entered.

"Hello, Chief," he said. "Nothing to report, no rescue calls and just a couple of routine radios.

They're here on the desk. How is Curly coming along?"

"He's doing fine," Becker rumbled as he picked up the radio messages and started to read them.

"Will his knee be all right?"

"What? His knee? Yes, I think so," Becker replied in an abstracted voice as his eyes ran over the typed lines.

"His knee is recovering very nicely, Jake," MacAlpin said. "They have taken a new set of X-rays and find that, while there was considerable trauma of the soft structures, there was no serious bone or ligamentary injury. He will be in the hospital for another month or so and he will have to use his leg with caution for another period, but there seems to be little doubt of his eventual recovery."

"That's fine, Mr. MacAlpin. I'll go visit him on my next liberty."

"I can assure you that your visit will be a welcome one. Despite the fascination of a blond nurse —who will never see fifty again—he is bored. He even welcomed the sight of my homely visage and endured without visible signs of torment, the inanities of my conversation for an hour. By all means, go and see him."

"That I'll do, Mr. MacAlpin."

The sound of the dinner bell rang through the

station and Becker dropped the radios he had finished reading on his desk.

"Come on, Jeff, let's wash up a bit. Jake, tell Hooky we'll be there in a minute."

"Okay, Chief, I'll tell him."

When Becker and MacAlpin entered the dining room, the crew of the station were standing behind their chairs. Becker lowered his bulk into the chair at the head of the table and there was a scraping of chairs as the crew seated themselves. Becker bowed his head.

"We ask Thy blessing, Oh, Lord, on these gifts which we are about to receive from Thy bounty. Amen," he rumbled. "Hooky, give Mr. MacAlpin a double order of beans, he's hungry." His eyes swept the table, mentally checking the crew. "Where's Corey?" he asked.

"He went for a walk along the beach with Surfman," the cook replied. "They left about half an hour ago."

"Didn't he know it was getting toward supper time?"

"Yes, sir, but he don't like chili beans much. He said he'd go by Sandy's place and get himself a sandwich and a coke. He'll be back in time to go on tower watch and I promised to save him a hunk of pie. How's Curly coming along, Chief?"

"He's doing fine, Hooky. He sent his best to all

Missing

of you and he'd like to see any of you next time you take liberty in Norfolk. He'll be in the hospital another month or so, but he's doing all right."

There was a murmur of satisfaction at the news. Becker turned to MacAlpin.

"It was right nice of Old Joey to go in to see him yesterday," he said. "Too bad I didn't know he wanted to go, I could have taken him in the jeep, today."

"That would have been a thoughtful gesture, Merle, and one worthy of your greatness of heart. Heart, I said, not girth. Joey, for some reason, has taken an abnormal liking to Morgan."

"Yeah, they seem right friendly."

"It is not only that, Merle, it transcends ordinary friendship. Morgan seems to have a fascination for Joey. Haven't you noticed that when they are together, Joey will sit for half an hour staring at Morgan's face?"

"Yeah, he does seem to look at Curly a lot."

"It is not mere looking, as you so baldly put it, Merle, it is a gaze so intent as to almost suggest hypnosis. Mingled with that, there is an intense struggle, as though Joey were fighting with himself."

"You sure see a lot, Jeff, if you can see stuff like that in as stupid a face as Old Joey's."

"Joey's face is far from stupid. It is blank. Stupidity would infer an inability to think, to have ever thought. Blankness, however, indicates merely an absence of thought at the present time."

"I don't see the difference. If he doesn't think, he doesn't think, and that's all there is to it, so far as I can see."

"There is a tremendous difference, Merle, as even the most elementary student of psychology would tell you. A man who cannot think must, perforce, be devoid of brain power. One who merely fails to think may conceivably have the ability to do so, although the ability is lying dormant."

"You're talking way above my head, Jeff. I don't think Old Joey has any brain to speak of, not more than enough to fit out an ordinary sized gopher,* at best."

"I can't agree. It is my humble opinion that Old Joey has a brain, a very adequate and usable brain of considerable intelligence. Something has happened in the past to render that brain temporarily unusable, or, if usable, to prevent the conclusions reached by that brain from penetrating into his consciousness. There is a perpetual struggle going on, a struggle for recrudescence, and there is something about Morgan's appearance that stimulates that struggle. At times it almost seems as though the brain were winning, but the stimulus is not suffi-

---

* a land turtle, noted for its stupidity.

ciently powerful and the defeated brain returns to the shadowland where, I believe, it still survives with much of its old power."

"You're way beyond me, Jeff."

"I'm way beyond myself, Merle, possibly beyond the present limits of psychological knowledge, but it is an interesting problem and one that some day I hope to see solved."

"I hope it is, Jeff, if you want it that way. Meanwhile, how about a game of checkers after supper? I'll give you some problems to solve."

"That is something I have learned to expect when I offer up my limited ability as a checker player as a sacrifice on the altar of your skill. However, if you will make good your promise to see that Mike's ravenous appetite is temporarily sated, I will come as a lamb to the slaughter."

"I'll send Hooky up with something as soon as supper's over. How about some more beans?"

"Always the things of the flesh appeal to your nature more strongly than do the things of the spirit. I mourn for the slight vestiges of your youthful figure that you still retain, Merle, and while mourning, I will join you in another helping of Hooky's beans."

When the meal was finished, Becker and MacAlpin adjourned to the recreation room where the checker board was waiting. Jeff Davis had spoken slightingly of his skill at the game, but his modesty fooled no one. Most of the crew gathered around the table to watch the protracted and bitterly fought battle they knew would ensue. The two men were past masters of the game and each knew that a single moment of relaxation or a single careless move would be triumphantly seized upon by his opponent and exploited to the limit. Oblivious to their surroundings and heedless of the passage of time, they sat intent on their game, each of them striving to fathom the meaning of each move of his opponent and to devise some strategy which would trap him into an unfavorable position.

The evening hours passed slowly. So engrossed were the two men that when the office telephone rang, it was forced to repeat its summons twice before Becker roused himself enough from his concentration to notice it.

"Answer that, will you, Jake?" he said. "Call me if it's anything that needs action."

Holman was back in a few moments.

"It was Barron, up in the tower, Chief," he reported. "It's five minutes past time for his relief and no one has shown up yet."

"Who's due on?"

"Corey Bassett."

"Where's Corey? Oh, I remember. Hasn't he got back yet?"

Missing 167

"No, sir. He's been gone over three hours."

"Where was he going? Sandy's, didn't Hooky say?"

"That he did, Chief."

"I reckon he got to talking and forgot he was due on. Well, I'll give him an extra shift so he'll remember another time. Tell Barron to stay there for half an hour and then, if Corey hasn't shown up, let Herb relieve him. It's your move, Jeff."

He turned back to the game. As he did so, there was a muffled barking at the front door of the station, then a scratching sound, followed by a renewed barking. "That's Surfman," Becker said. "Corey'll be here in a minute. Let the fool dog in, somebody, before he tears the door down."

Surfman was barking steadily and scratching at the station door. Herb Scarsdale rose and left the recreation room. A moment later he was back, the big Chesapeake bounding along beside him. Surfman was still barking and was leaping up at Scarsdale, demanding his attention.

"What's the matter, Surfman? Get down, don't jump up on me like that. What's the matter with you?"

Surfman dropped to a crouch, but looked up and barked steadily in a muffled tone.

"What's that you've got, Surfman?" Scarsdale asked, reaching down for a white object gripped in the dog's teeth. "Hey, let go. What you got, anyway?"

Surfman refused to relinquish the object he was carrying and a fresh volley of barks came from him. He made no attempt to jerk away and allowed Scarsdale to examine the article, but he did not loosen his grip on it.

"Say, Chief!" Scarsdale cried. "Surfman's got Corey's hat."

"Yeah?" Becker looked up absently from the game. "Let him have it. He won't hurt it."

Surfman jumped to his feet and raced toward the door, barking vociferously and looking back over his shoulder as if asking for someone to follow him.

"Chief, something's wrong!" Scarsdale cried. "Watch the way that dog's acting."

Becker divorced his attention from the game.

"Come here, Surfman," he rumbled.

The Chesapeake came forward promptly but when Becker reached for the white hat in the dog's jaws, Surfman would not give it up. Instead, he bounded away toward the door, barking anxiously.

"Something *is* wrong, Merle," MacAlpin exclaimed. "Bassett is in some sort of trouble and Surfman wants to take us to him."

"I believe you're right, Jeff," Becker replied as he watched the dog's actions. "I'm going to follow him and see what's wrong. Jake, you and Herb come with me. Have Barron stay in the tower until we get back, no matter how late it is." He hesitated a moment. "Better get a litter, Jake," he went on. "I hope we won't need it, but we might."

"I'm going too, Merle," MacAlpin said.

"Okay, if you want to, Jeff, but if we go along the wash, it's going to be a rough trip. The tide's almost in."

"Surfman may not take us along the wash, there's no telling where Bassett is. At any rate, I'm going. If it gets too tough, I can always turn back."

"Suit yourself. Surfman, let me have that hat."

As soon as he was certain that the men were going to follow him, Surfman readily gave up the hat which he had kept firmly gripped in his jaws. Becker looked inside and gave a grunt.

"It's Corey's hat, all right. Well, get the lead out of your pants and come on with that litter. If anything's wrong, we haven't over a week, you know. If there isn't—"

The tone of his voice did not bode well for Corey Bassett.

The Search

As Becker opened the front door of the station, Surfman bounded out into the darkness. He dashed away in the direction of the beach and in a moment was lost to sight.

"Here, this won't do!" Becker rumbled. "Surfman, come back here. *Surfman!*"

The call had hardly left his lips before the Chesapeake was back, bounding around them eagerly, then once more racing off into the darkness before he could be caught.

"We'll have to catch him and put him on a leash," Becker said. "If we don't, we'll soon lose him and won't know where to go. Jake, get a short length of heaving line."

"I don't think we'll need it, Merle," MacAlpin said. "That dog has lots of sense. He's asking us to follow him and I'm sure he'll keep in touch with us."

"Get the line anyway, Jake. We'll try to follow him without it, but I'd rather have it along."

Before Holman could return with the line, Surfman was back, barking with fresh intensity and very evidently begging them to follow him, but when Becker essayed to catch him, he bounded away into the impenetrable darkness of the night.

"Let's go," Becker said when Holman came out. "Surfman, where are you?"

A quick bark from the darkness answered him and the group of four men started toward the sound.

"He's evidently heading right across the swamp," Becker said doubtfully. "I think we'd better take the trail to the wash."

"We'd better follow the dog, Merle," MacAlpin said. "For all we know, Bassett might be in the swamp. Surfman is the only one who has any idea where we're going."

"Reckon that's sense, Jeff, but I wish he'd take a better road, if he can."

With Becker's flashlight picking out the ground before them, the group plunged forward. In a hundred yards they came to the edge of the swamp which separated the station from the ridge along the beach. Becker hesitated a moment at the edge of the low ground, but Surfman's bark came from directly ahead, so with a grunt of disgust, he entered the knee-deep stagnant water and splashed his way forward.

Surfman kept a few yards ahead of them. At times Becker could pick up his glowing eyes in the beam of the flashlight, but at other times they had only the sound of his splashing progress to guide them. Despite the recent rains the water over the low ground was not deep and the sand underfoot was firm. It was quickly evident that Surfman was not taking a direct route to the beach, but was picking his way, avoiding the deeper holes of the swamp.

It took them some time to cover the half mile that separated the station from the beach and when they climbed over the low ridge which edged the wash, Becker gave an exclamation of disgust.

"I thought we should have taken the trail," he said.

"As usual, Merle, your hunches prove superior to the cold processes of logical thought," MacAlpin replied. "However, I believe we have saved some time."

Becker did not reply, but turned south along the narrow wash to follow the dog. The tide was almost in and only a few yards separated the edge of the surf from the low ridge which marked the limits of the beach. In another half hour the waves would be lapping against the ridge and the wash would disappear until the receding tide uncovered it.

The Search

As they neared the point of Cape Hatteras, the going got steadily harder. The wash was growing narrower by the minute and the upper edge of the beach was littered with debris. Although Becker and MacAlpin, who were leading the way with flashlights, could avoid much of it, Holman and Scarsdale were less fortunate. To add to the difficulties, Surfman, once they started along the wash, ranged well ahead and refused to come close enough to Becker to allow himself to be captured and leashed.

"I hope it isn't more than twenty miles farther," Becker rumbled in his deep voice.

He had hardly voiced the wish when a sudden loud burst of barking came from the darkness, a hundred yards ahead of them. The barking had a note of excitement and urgency which it had not previously held. The four men broke into a run. The barking ceased after a moment, then came again in a muffled tone. A few moments later the beams of the lights picked out the dog. Surfman was standing in the edge of the surf, bracing himself and tugging at a body, striving to drag it up the beach until it would be beyond the reach of the lapping waves.

"It's Corey, all right!" Becker cried as his light flashed over the scene.

In a moment strong hands had lifted the body and carried it back up on the ridge, well beyond the reach of the waves. Becker handed his flashlight to Holman and bent over the recumbent form, his ear to Bassett's chest. He listened intently for a minute, then stood erect.

"He's breathing," he announced, "But his heart sounds pretty faint. He must have had a wallop. Give me the light, Jake."

He turned the beam of the light on Bassett's head and examined it carefully, but there was no sign of a bump or cut that would account for the Coastguardsman's unconsciousness.

"Maybe he had a stroke," Scarsdale suggested. "My grandfather had one and he looked that way."

"Could be," Becker rumbled.

"I don't think so, Merle," MacAlpin, who had been studying the unconscious man's face, said. "I think it's more likely to be a heart attack than a stroke, judging from the pallor and general appearance. However, the cause of his condition is immaterial at present, the thing important is the action to be taken."

"We'll take him to the station," Becker said. A moment of doubt struck him and he turned to MacAlpin. "What do you think about it, Jeff? We can't do anything for him here."

"I'm afraid he must be taken to the station," MacAlpin replied slowly, "although it would be better, if possible, to bring aid here rather than to take him to aid. But the important thing is to get medical care for him with the least delay, and that means phoning Norfolk and having a doctor flown here."

"We won't get a doctor tonight," Becker said. "A plane can't land on the wash with the tide in and no pilot would try to set a plane down on the flats in the middle of the night."

"No, but there's a helicopter in Elizabeth City and they can use it. Wait a minute, though. There's a doctor in Buxton."

"Who?"

"Mary Green's brother. He practices in Raleigh but he is visiting her now. We can send a car for him as soon as we get to the station."

"We can do better than that," Becker said. "Jake, take one of the lights and start for Buxton on a run. Turn that doctor out and bring him to the station. He ought to get there as soon as we do."

"Can you manage the litter—"

"Don't worry about that, you get going. Jeff, you and Herb can take the head and I'll handle the foot. Open the litter and we'll get him on it. All right, Surfman, you've done your bit, and a dandy bit it was. Now, get out of the way."

The four men carefully lifted the unconscious

Bassett onto the litter. Jake Holman sped away into the darkness toward the Hatteras-Avon highway.

"Carry him as steadily and evenly as you can," MacAlpin warned. "If it's what I suspect, a shaking up won't help him any."

"Think we'd better head for the highway, Jeff? It would be evener going."

"No, I believe not, Merle. It's a great many miles farther that way and we've got to get him to the station eventually in any case. There is no place to put him in Buxton."

"All right, we'll go along the wash. Ready? Lift."

The litter was raised and the three men started the long carry, MacAlpin using the one light they had to pick out the smoothest possible road. Surfman, content that he had done his part, paced sedately along in the rear.

"You were right, Jeff," Becker said as he entered the recreation room two hours later. "Dr. Estevan says it was a heart attack. I've talked with the Duty Officer at District and there will be an ambulance plane dispatched in the morning to take him to the Marine Hospital."

"Is it wise to move him that soon?"

"The doctor says it's best. The trip won't be too hard on him by plane and he's got to have steady medical care for some time."

The Search

"Can't Dr. Estevan take care of him, at least for the present?"

"No, he's heading back for Raleigh. He planned to go on the bus in the morning, but he'll wait 'til Bassett is taken away, then I'll run him in to Manteo in the jeep. He says Surfman saved Corey's life. If we had been a couple of hours later finding him, it would have been just too bad."

"A couple of hours later we would not have found him, Merle. Remember, the tide was almost up to the ridge when we got there. In fact, Surfman dragged him out of the water as we came up. If we had been two hours later, the tide would have come in and floated him, then, as it turned, it would have carried him out to sea."

"That it would, Jeff. I hadn't considered that."

"Once out to sea, a shark would have got him, or he might have floated for days, even out into the Gulf Stream. In that case, his body would never have been found."

"Air Search and Rescue would probably have found him, Jeff."

"If they had been sent out, they might have. But, would they have been sent out?"

"Of course. Why not?"

"Why should they? If Bassett had not returned, you would have started hunting for him. You would probably have found that he had been at Sandy's and had a sandwich. There you would have lost all trace of him. What would have been your next step?"

Becker pondered the problem.

"I'd notify the Group Commander at Oregon Inlet and then I'd have done whatever Mr. Hargrove said to do."

"Precisely. Probably nothing would have been done for several days, expecting that he would show up. When he didn't, even if you suspected what had happened to him, which you probably wouldn't, you would have no clue leading to the open sea. Probably several more days would be lost in searching the island with bloodhounds. By that time, if Search and Rescue planes were sent out, they would be behind the eight ball with thousands of square miles to search and the chances for success infinitesimal."

"I reckon as how you're right, Jeff."

"And in the final analysis, what action would be taken after a month or more of search proved fruitless? What action was taken in the last case of this sort at the Cape Hatteras Station?"

"There never was one, so far as I know."

"There was one, Merle, although it was before your time here. Think back over the old station records. Think of March 16, 1929, to be exact."

"I was at Ocracoke then," Becker said. "Say,

wasn't that the night that Chief Davidson of Little Kinnakeet was lost?"

"It was, and it was also the night that Surfman Stanton Truslow disappeared from Cape Hatteras. He, you may remember, was dropped from the rolls of the Coast Guard as a deserter."

"That he was, Jeff."

"He went off on patrol that night and he had no dog with him to bring back his hat and word that he was in trouble. Isn't it possible that history is repeating herself and what happened to Bassett tonight is what happened to Truslow twenty years ago?"

"I reckon it is, Jeff."

"I think we have Surfman to thank, not only for Bassett's life—if he lives—but also for keeping another blot off the station record. I think, if I were you, I would recommend to Norfolk that he be appointed a Chief Boatswain's Mate (Lifesaving) and given command of a station. From what I've seen of his judgment, he would be an improvement on some of the Chiefs we now have."

"Especially the Chief at Cape Hatteras?" Becker chuckled.

"I didn't say that, Merle, but at least he keeps his figure trim and his weight down to reasonable proportions."

Becker's huge frame shook with laughter.

"It isn't fair to pick on me, Jeff," he protested. "I eat almost nothing and you know it. I get up from the table hungry after every meal."

"Which is a good thing or the Coast Guard would have to ask the Congress for a special appropriation for the purpose of feeding you. Well, the witching hour of dawn approaches and I must hie me to my palatial abode. I'm sleepy."

"So am I, Jeff, but I think I'll stay up the rest of the night. I want to keep an eye on Bassett."

"I would share your vigil, Merle, were it not for the fact that I believe I would soon be slumbering in a chair and wake with my aged and decrepit muscles tied in bow knots. Besides, Mike has doubtless already digested the sustenance which you so kindly sent up for him and will shortly be yowling for more."

"You sure think a lot of that cat, Jeff."

"No, I do not, and he has a correspondingly poor opinion of my character and amiability. Mike is both an individualist and a philosopher, and I, in my humble way, strive to attain to those heights. We tolerate one another on the sole basis of our mutual opinion of the frailty of the balance of humanity. Good night."

"Good night, Jeff. Can't I run you up in the jeep?"

"No, my bones have taken enough punishment

for one day and I decline to subject them to more of your driving. Good night, Surfman, even at the risk of adding, if possible, to Mike's disgust with me, I will return with your odor on my hands."

Surfman wagged his tail and accompanied MacAlpin to the door.

Joey Tries To Remember

SURFMAN SAT on the station porch with a disconsolate air, his gaze fixed on the winding trail which led to the highway. It had been more than two months since his master had gone away and the time had seemed like an eternity to the Chesapeake. He had not lacked for attention from the other members of the station crew, especially since the night when his prompt action had been instrumental in saving Corey Bassett's life. He was pampered, petted and deferred to in a way that would have turned the head of any less stable-minded dog, but, while Surfman delighted in the attention he received and was always ready to accompany any of the crew on a hike or to go out on one of the station boats, most of his unoccupied time was spent on the front porch, staring down the road and hoping for his master's return.

Barron Migert came out of the station, a coil of shot line looped over his shoulder. He stopped to rumple Surfman's ears and stroke his head.

"Still looking for your boss, Surfman?" he said. "Cheer up, he'll be back soon now. Yes, sir, he'll be back soon, almost any day now. I'm going to the shed and fake this line in a shot line box. Want to help me? Come on Surfman, you can help, or at least you can boss the job. Come on, boy."

Surfman thumped his tail at the caress and when Migert started on, he rose and followed him. They had gone but a few steps when the Chesapeake stopped dead in his tracks and once more stared up the trail. His keen ears had caught the sound of a car which had turned off the highway. He stood rigid, his head thrust forward and his ears erect. A command car was swaying and bumping along the trail toward the station. As it came near, Surfman went slowly forward to meet it, his tail moving slowly in a tentative welcome. Suddenly his tail broke into a frenzy of activity and a deep-toned bark came from his throat. He dashed forward and capered crazily about, striving to climb into the car. A vagrant puff of wind had brought to his sensitive nostrils the odor for which he had sought so patiently for months.

"Hello, Surfman," came Curly's cheerful voice. "Hello, old fellow. Yes, sir, good dog. Hey, look out, fellow! Get down, you goon, this leg is still tender. Down, Surfman, *down*, I say!"

The dog obediently dropped to a crouch, his tail hammering the sand violently, but as his master climbed out of the command car, he could restrain himself no longer. Barking wildly, he capered about, then leaped up on his master, licking at his hands and striving to reach his face. With a laugh, Curly leaned against the car and devoted his attention to fondling the excited dog.

"Hello, Curly," Merle Becker's deep voice rumbled from the station porch. "Glad to have you back. Come aboard."

"Hello, Chief," Curly cried. "I'm glad to be back, believe you me. Surfman, behave yourself, you'll knock me down if you're not careful. Down, Surfman!"

The Chesapeake dropped again to a crouch and Curly turned to the driver of the command car.

"Toss out my stuff, will you?" he asked. "Give me that small bag first. Here, Surfman, take this, it'll keep you busy."

The dog gripped the handle of the bag in his strong jaws and quivered with eagerness, waiting for further orders.

"Here, Curly, let me get that stuff," Barron Migert said as he dropped the coil of shot line and came quickly forward.

"Thanks, Barron, I think I will. This knee of mine is still just a speck tender."

"How is it, Curly, is it coming along all right?"

"Oh, it's doing fine, Barron. I really never know I have it unless I put a strain on it some way. The sawbones says it'll be as good as new in another month or even less if I exercise it regularly and avoid straining it."

"Gee, that's fine, Curly. We're sure glad to see you back."

"I'm afraid I won't be good for much but tower watch and things like that for a while," Curly said with a grin. "I've got the habit of gold-bricking in the hospital and that's an easy habit to get and a hard one to lose. My knee will make me sort of a prima donna around here."

"We'll find plenty to keep you busy," Becker rumbled. "I've got a message for you. Old Joey has been here a dozen times asking about you and he wants you to go fishing with him as soon as you can."

"That's swell, Chief. Joey was in to Norfolk to see me three times and he told me he was going to take me out as soon as I could go. But, of course, I don't want any liberty until I've caught up on my work a little. How about me standing two, or three, tower watches a day for the next week or two? That'll give the rest of the boys a little break and I'm supposed to favor this knee for a month or so."

"We'll see," Becker replied. "I promised Joey I'd let you go out as soon as you got back." He turned to the driver of the command car. "You'll stay here tonight, won't you?"

"Thanks, Chief, but I can't. I've got to shove off right away and catch the last ferry at Oregon Inlet."

"You're welcome to stay, we serve pretty good chow here."

"I'd like to stay, Chief, but I've got to pick up some letters at Kill Devil Hills Station and get back to Norfolk tonight. Thanks for the invite."

"You're welcome any time. Give my best to Chief Silvas."

"I'll do that, Chief. Be seeing you."

He backed the command car around and drove off. Curly, flanked by Becker and Migert who were carrying his bags, entered the station, Surfman with the small bag gripped in his teeth, following closely.

Despite Becker's promise to Joey, it was almost a month before Curly felt free to take a day on liberty to go fishing, and then it was Jeff Davis MacAlpin who forced the issue.

It was late fall and the season of high gales was at hand. Already several readings of Force 8* or

---
* Gale force, 34 to 40 nautical miles per hour. See Appendix IV

higher had been recorded and these were a mere promise of still higher and more violent winds to come. The crew were busy readying the station for the winter weather, weather in which rescue calls, if they came, would be emergency ones. For the first week Curly contented himself with standing tower watch, relieving the other men for heavier work, but as his knee steadily improved, he began to do his share of the other work and by the end of the month he was doing full duty. The only evidence of his injury that anyone could notice was a certain care and deliberation he exercised when it came to climbing or to other strains on his leg. Even this care, as he freely admitted, was dictated more by caution and a hope of avoiding a fresh injury than by any actual necessity or weakness in his knee.

"Morgan," MacAlpin said one night, nearly a month after Curly's return from the hospital, "I am disappointed in you."

"What about, Mr. MacAlpin?" Curly asked in surprise. "What have I done now?"

"It is not a sin of commission, Morgan, it is a sin of omission that earns my disapprobation. It shows a distinct trait of selfishness in your character to neglect your friends."

"But I haven't—"

"You distinctly have. While you languished forlorn on your bed of pain in Norfolk, Old Joey made three trips into Norfolk to visit you. They were trips which Joey could ill afford, from a pecuniary standpoint. Also, it was the first time since he has lived here that he has been off Hatteras Island, except in his fishing boat, more than once a year. All that he has asked of you in return has been that you go fishing with him, yet you have neglected him utterly since your return."

"Gosh, Mr. MacAlpin, we've been so busy here—"

"That, my boy, is a very lame and inadequate excuse. I am sure that Merle would have excused you for that purpose at any time you had asked him to."

"That I would," Becker rumbled. "I've offered him liberty half a dozen times since he's been back."

"I know, but the boys had to do my work for a couple of months and I wanted—"

"Evidence of that sort comes under the head of mitigating circumstances and tends to affect only the sentence, not the finding. The jury finds you guilty as charged. Before I pass sentence, not only evidence of your past good intentions, but also evidence of your future intentions will be given due consideration. Prisoner at the bar, speak up. What are you going to do about it?"

"Gosh, Mr. MacAlpin, I've meant to go. I'll be glad to go—any time."

"Would tomorrow be a suitable day on which to repair your omission?"

"He can have liberty if he wants it," Becker rumbled.

"I'll take his tower watch," Wyman Ballard volunteered. "He's taken my last four for me."

"I'll drive him to Avon in the jeep tomorrow morning," Herb Scarsdale offered.

"I'll get him in the evening," Bill Darrow chimed in.

"I'll fix him a lunch," was Hooky's contribution.

"And the weather report predicts a calm sea," MacAlpin said. "No excuse left, Morgan."

"Why, sure I'll go. I'd like to go, it's just that—"

"Merle," MacAlpin interrupted. "Will you call Little Kinnakeet and ask Chief Scarsdale to find Old Joey and tell him that Morgan will be at his boat in the early dawn tomorrow, prepared to fish throughout the day? If, for any reason, he can't deliver the message, he can call back."

"That I'll do, Jeff," Becker replied as he heaved his bulk up from his chair and started for the office. "It's time Curly took a day off."

"He and Surfman both," MacAlpin replied. "They've both been sticking around the station too close."

Light was just beginning to show in the east when the jeep pulled up at the dock in Avon where Joey kept his boat. There was no wind but the air was raw and cold and Curly was glad of the forethought which had caused him to don a heavy sweater under his windbreaker before leaving the station. There was no one in sight on the dock, but as Surfman bounded to the ground, there was a hail from the *Nemo*. Surfman barked in reply and Joey jumped from his boat to the dock.

"Hello, Curly," he greeted his guest. "I sure was glad to get that word last night, although I'm afraid it's not going to be a very good day for sport."

He cast an experienced eye aloft.

"May be a capful of wind later," he said, "but I don't reckon it'll get rough. Might be we'll get a flurry of snow, sky looks like it."

"That won't worry me," Curly grinned as he gripped Joey's hand. "I'm sorry it's been so long, but we've been really busy at the station."

"Didn't want to get in the way," Joey said, "but I did want you to go with me one day before the weather got bad. All ready to go?"

"All ready, Joey. Here's a flock of sandwiches Hooky fixed for us. My rod's in the jeep. I'll get it."

With Surfman at his heels, he boarded the *Nemo* and a few minutes later the little fishing boat was chugging her way through the Avon channel to the sound. Curly rigged his rod and as they cleared the channel, tossed a feather squid overboard and settled himself on a stool in the well deck. Surfman put his paws on the after rail and stared intently at the boat's wake.

"I doubt we'll get much, Surfman," Curly said. "It's pretty late in the year for trolling."

"That it is," Joey said, giving the wheel a spin. "We'll go out a piece and drop a trawl line with barrel floats. Might get a mess that-a-way."

The *Nemo* chugged steadily along. Curly relaxed his attention and turned to speak to Joey. Before he could speak there was a sharp tug on his line, followed by a volley of excited barks from Surfman.

"*Strike!*" Curly shouted as he lifted the point of his rod and tightened his star drag. Joey cut the motor of the *Nemo* and was beside his guest in an instant.

"What you got, Curly?" he asked.

"Oh, something small. It might be a bonita, it fights like one, but it's no size."

The fish made a quick preliminary run, but the battle was short-lived. As Curly began to wind in his reel, the fish gave up the struggle and came toward the boat with little resistance. Surfman watched eagerly. The catch was within ten yards of the boat when a long fin cut the water just behind it. A moment later there was a tug that bent the sturdy rod sharply and the line began to run rapidly off the reel.

"Shark!" Curly cried as he tightened the drag to the limit he dared with a fifteen thread line. "Follow him or he'll run my line right off."

Joey started the *Nemo's* motor and turned the boat to follow the fish, pushing the little boat to the limit of her speed, but his best efforts were of no avail. Yard by yard the line faded off the reel as the shark kept up its rush with undiminished speed. Curly tightened his drag again in a final effort to check the headlong rush of the fish. The tip of the rod flew upward and the line went slack.

"He's gone," Curly said as he began to retrieve his line. "He was a big one, too."

"Wouldn't have been worth nothing except for his liver if you'd got him," Joey consoled his guest. "Like as not we could never have boated him, even if you got him alongside."

"I hate to lose my line," Curly said ruefully. "I haven't got a spare."

The line had parted some thirty yards from the reel and Curly knew that his trolling was over for the day. Joey had no line light enough for use on a reel, so Curly laid his rod aside and helped Joey bait the long trawl line which the fisherman proposed to drop overboard.

Once baited, one end of the line was fastened to a barrel float which Joey tossed over. The *Nemo* chugged slowly ahead while Curly paid out the trawl line from which hung six hundred short lines, each terminating in a hook baited with a strip of cut fish. When the line was out, the *Nemo's* motor was stopped and the little craft wallowed gently in the sea. An hour or more would pass before they would go back along the line, removing any fish and rebaiting stripped hooks, preparatory to another setting of the line.

"We might as well have a sandwich," Curly remarked, opening the package. "Hooky sent plenty, and a bone for Surfman too. Here, Joey, help yourself."

The fisherman took one of the sandwiches and for a few minutes they ate in silence.

"You're feeling pretty good today, Joey," Curly remarked, his mouth full of sandwich.

"I feel fine," Joey assured him. "I do most times. It's just when things get confused, sort of, that I don't feel good. It seems then like I see things—"

An expression, almost of fright, crossed his face and he shuddered.

"What sort of things, Joey?" Curly asked quietly, although his heart was pounding hard.

Joey passed his hand over his face and rubbed his eyes.

"I—I don't know," he confessed and his voice had lost some of the clearness which had marked it.

"It just seems like—I don't know. They're things . . ."

His voice trailed off into silence. Curly restrained his eager desire to ask further questions and waited. When Joey spoke again, his voice was low, almost a mumble.

"I see—things," he said. "They're bad. They come for me. I can't tell what they want— They want me —they're after me. If I could just remember. They're just out there—" he waved his hand in an aimless circle— "They won't come closer— They—"

Again his voice trailed off into an unintelligible jumble of sound. Joey's face was strained as he battled to capture the obscure vision that floated just beyond his reach. Twice he seemed on the point of winning the battle, but the flash of intelligence quickly faded each time. He was silent for ten minutes. At last he rubbed his face and looked up. When he spoke his voice was again normal.

"I don't know, Curly," he said, "and that's what worries me so. I don't know where I came from or how I got here. I must have been hurt—or something—I can't seem to remember. Sometimes at night I see things and know what happened, but then I wake up and I don't know. It's—bad."

"It must be tough," Curly said sympathetically, "but I wouldn't worry too much, Joey. After all, you have your friends and you're getting along all right. What does it matter what may have happened years ago?"

"It matters," Joey said stubbornly. "There's something I must remember—and tell, but I—I can't remember. Sometimes I think I'm going to. When I see you, it almost comes to me, but before I can get it straight in my mind, it goes away again, and I—I can't remember. And I try—I try."

Tears trickled out from under his eyelids and ran down his tanned and weather-beaten face. Surfman edged forward and licked sympathetically at his hand. Curly was embarrassed by the show of emotion, but he spoke in a quiet, soothing tone.

"I think you try too hard to remember, Joey," he said. "Just let it go and don't worry about it. Then, some day you'll remember everything."

"You think so, Curly?" Joey's voice was pathetic in its eagerness.

"Of course I do."

"I—I hope so. It seems that I— I must—"

"You will, Joey, just don't worry about it. What say we run the line? I think we've got some fish on it."

"Sure thing, Curly. You haul and I'll rebait and coil."

Only five small fish were taken from the line, although many of the hooks had been stripped, presumably by crabs. When the line was on board

Joey headed the *Nemo* south and went a mile along the coast before making a second set.

The day passed slowly. Joey did his best, but the fish were few in number and small in size. When they headed back for Avon with the approach of evening, the catch was hardly large enough to pay for the gasoline they had used. Surfman, who had shown intense interest while his master was trolling, had watched the hauling of the trawl line the first time, then had lost interest and had spent the day curled up in the well deck, sleeping.

"It's been a fine day, Joey, and Surfman and I both thank you," Curly said as the *Nemo* ran alongside the Avon dock.

"I hope you'll come again," Joey said, a trace of wistfulness in his voice. "Maybe next time the fishing will be better."

"Of course we'll go again, Joey, any time you ask us—and I can get liberty. I'll bring a spare line next time."

"Take these fish with you, Curly. They aren't many, but might be they'll make a mess for the boys."

Curly was about to protest, but a glance at Joey's eager face changed his mind.

"Sure thing, Joey, and thanks a lot for them. Can't you come to the station for supper tomorrow?

I'll come and get you in the jeep. Hooky will cook these fish and we'd like to have you."

"I'd—I'd rather—not."

"Just as you like, Joey, but you'd be mighty welcome. Well, thanks again, and I'll see you soon."

"Please come again," Joey said. "Sometimes when I see you, I—I almost remember. I think—you were in—you are part of—you—I don't remember," he finished lamely in a halting voice.

"Well, just don't worry about it, Joey, and some day it'll all come back. I'm afraid I'm not part of it, though. Whatever it was, it must have happened before I was born."

"No, you're in it—you are— I see you sometimes —so clear—I know—I— Good night, Curly, and God bless you."

"Good night, Joey, and thanks for a swell day. Come on, Surfman, we'll be late for supper if we don't move out."

Surfman barked joyously and ran toward the waiting jeep.

Hurricane

THE WINTER STORMS off Cape Hatteras were in full swing. They started in late December and, as January wore on, they increased, both in frequency and in violence. In the early part of February there was a break in the weather, a period of light winds and mild temperatures, but the weather-wise Becker was lulled to no false sense of security.

"She's just easing up to get a better holt," he said, looking with a critical eye at the deceptively clear sky. "There's just about so much wind going to blow every year. Leastwise, that's how I figure it. If we don't get it now, we'll get it later."

"You think we'll have a bad March, Chief?"

"March is always bad," Becker rumbled. "You've got to expect that, but this weather won't hold to March. Wouldn't surprise me none if we had a real wingding any day now. If the wind shifts to the northeast, she's likely to come boiling in at ninety miles an hour."

Curly gave a low whistle.

"I've seen her worse than that here. In the old sailing days, a wind like that would mean two or three wrecks piled up on the beach, but wind don't mean so much any more. First place, every ship has radio. Once they get a storm warning, they go out to where they have plenty of sea room. Second place, if a storm does catch them, they've got plenty power to stay off the beach and away from Diamond Shoals. About the only thing in much danger nowadays is fishing boats and such small craft, and they stay close to harbor or don't go out at all when storm warnings are flying. We haven't had anything big come ashore since the *City of Roseville* broke her propeller shaft and went on the beach near Ocracoke. That was six years ago last month."

"I guess that's true everywhere, Chief. I've never seen the beach apparatus used, except at drill."

"You'd better hope you never do, but we've got to keep it ready. Did you grease the blocks on the service cart yesterday like I asked you?"

"Yes, sir, the blocks and the hawser cutter and the reels. And I polished the Lyle gun too."

"That's good. If you get time today, you'd better exercise the tractor. It hasn't been out of the shed for more than a week."

"I'll do that right away, Chief. Come on, Surfman, get moving. We've got work to do."

With the Chesapeake at his heels, Curly started for the tractor shed.

Despite Becker's gloomy prognostications, the fair weather held for two weeks and it was not until the twenty-third of February that a change came. Then the wind, which had blown steadily from the southwest, shifted around to the north and began to increase steadily in force. Hourly the readings of the anemometer grew higher. Storm warning flags were hoisted and the fishing boats which had ventured out scurried back to the safety of the harbors, there to lie at anchor during the storm which the weather forecast told was coming down from the Newfoundland Banks.

At the station the crew busied themselves bolting on the hurricane shutters and combing the grounds to make sure that all loose articles were stowed away in buildings or were securely lashed in place. At the white house near the old light Jeff Davis MacAlpin and Old Joey, who was spending the night with him, busied themselves with similar activity. Nor were they alone in this. At Buxton, at Avon, at Hatteras and the other villages, men scurried around in preparation and by nightfall Hatteras Island was ready for the onset.

Fifty miles south, the Master of the seagoing tug *Lucy Arkwright* studied the weather report and scratched his head.

"Looks like we might have a right smart of wind tonight," he said to his mate. "Coming from the northeast too. We'll be driving straight into it."

The Mate looked back at the LST* which was wallowing along at the end of a steel towing hawser behind the tug.

"What's the forecast?" he asked.

"Whole gale," the Master replied. "Might run up to sixty with gusts higher."

"We won't make any northing in the teeth of that."

"No, best we can hope for is to hold position. We might be driven south a bit."

"Hadn't we better go into the Sound? Drum Inlet's not far ahead."

"What's the matter, Mister? Showing a yellow streak?"

The Mate flushed uncomfortably.

"No, sir, I just thought—"

"I do the thinking around here, Mister."

"Yes, sir."

"I wouldn't try to go through Drum Inlet with a tow at low tide and this much wind. We might get in through Ocracoke or Hatteras, but we won't try. There's a time penalty on this job and we're going ahead. Shift the course a point east, we can use plenty of sea room if this forecast is right."

---
* Landing Ship (Tank)

"Yes, sir."

The *Lucy Arkwright* veered to the east to go well outside Diamond Shoals and plowed steadily ahead, the LST wallowing along in her wake.

The storm arrived on schedule. All during the first half of the night the wind steadily freshened and the surf increased in violence until it was pounding against the ridge which separated the wash from the upper ground, hurling spray high into the air to be caught by the wind and carried far inland, dashing like rain against the buildings of the station.

Shortly after midnight the wind died away suddenly and there was a short interval of almost dead calm, during which the pounding of the surf was plainly audible. Then with a banshee howl, the storm struck and the watch tower quivered as if struck a blow. Higher and higher the note of the wind rose until at last there was a creaking, then a series of reports like pistol shots. A moment later there was a crash that brought every member of the crew awake. The station flagpole, calculated to withstand a wind stress of greater than a hundred and twenty miles an hour, had crashed to the ground, carrying with it in its fall the telephone line and shutting the station off from all communication with the outside world except by radio.

Under the force of the blow, the Diamond Shoals

Lightship heeled far over, tumbling her sleeping crew from their bunks. Over she went until her gunwale was only a few feet above the water, then she began slowly to right herself. She came up until she was again riding the waves, bobbing like a cork on the heavy swell with mighty waves crashing against her and sending tons of water rolling over her sloping deck. The watch off duty got back into their bunks and braced themselves as best they could against the erratic motion. The anchor watch made his way along the water-swept deck to inspect the chains. The anchors were holding and he breathed a prayer that they would not drag nor the anchor chains part, forcing the ship to either scurry to port or to ride out the storm at sea, leaving the dangerous shoals with no light or radio beacon to warn approaching ships.

The *Lucy Arkwright* was plowing along five miles east of Avon. The sturdy craft bored into the mountainous seas, shipping them over her bow, then shrugging them off as her prow lifted for another encounter. Behind her the bulk of the LST wallowed along, straining at the hawser which connected her to the tug. The wind struck the vessels with terrific force and the *Lucy Arkwright* staggered and slowed. Her engines throbbed steadily and her powerful screw labored, but she slowed almost to a standstill as the wind caught the high bow of the

LST and exerted its mighty force. Over the howling of the gale came a high singing note, the humming of the strained towing hawser. Then came a sharp ping, and then another. Suddenly the *Lucy Arkwright* bounded forward, burying her nose in an oncoming wave while her screw thrashed wildly in the air. There was a crash as the end of the parted hawser, coiling back like a striking snake, sheared off half of the tug's wheel house.

"God Awmighty!" gasped the helmsman.

The inrushing gale almost tore him from the wheel but he hung on in desperation and spun it frantically. Gradually the nose of the tug lifted and she answered to her helm. In another minute she was plowing steadily ahead, bucking the vicious waves and bobbing about erratically on the heavy swell. The half dazed helmsman jerked at the engine room telegraph and began to bellow down the speaking tube. The tug's engine slowed and she began to assume a more regular motion.

Aboard the LST the helmsman was, for a moment, unaware that the hawser had parted and that the ship was adrift. The short end of the broken hawser had flown back and thrashed the air, but had not struck the vessel with any force. The boat slowly lost headway and as she did so, the wind caught her high bow and started to swing her around. The helmsman fought with his wheel, trying to bring her head back into the wind, to keep her following steadily in the wake of the tug. As the LST lost headway, she no longer responded to her helm and the wheel spun easily and uselessly in the helmsman's hands. The vessel swung around until she was broadside to the wind and was wallowing in the trough of the waves. The helmsman abandoned his useless wheel and groped his way below.

"Skipper!" he bawled, hammering at the door of one of the cabins. "Furness! Turn out. We're adrift!"

"What?"

"We're adrift. Hawser's parted."

The cabin door opened and a half-clothed man stood in the doorway, his eyes stupid from sleep. A heavy roll of the LST threw him out of the doorway and he crashed against a bulkhead, wide awake.

"What's happened?" he snapped.

"We're adrift," the helmsman repeated for the third time. "The towing hawser must have parted."

"I'm going topside. Rouse the crew."

Captain Furness made his way to the wheel house with difficulty where he was shortly joined by the four members of the crew.

"We may have slipped the hawser, not parted it," Furness said. "See if it's still secured to the towing bitt."

One of the men made his way forward. When he

returned with word that the end of the hawser was still in place, all five men made their way to the bitt, but they quickly found they could accomplish nothing.

"Where did the *Lucy* go?" Furness fumed. "She could put another line aboard if she has a spare hawser. Oh, here she comes. Stand by to take a line."

Through the darkness they could see the lights of the tug nosing her way back toward them. She swung around the LST, approaching within a boat's length, her searchlight sweeping the deck and picking out Captain Furness, who braced himself against the forward gunwale. He waved and strove to shout into the storm, but the wind tore the words from his lips and he ceased as he realized the futility of his efforts.

A man appeared on the *Lucy Arkwright's* deck. He hung on with one hand while he swung his free arm in a circle. Suddenly his hand shot out but the end of the heaving line he had tried to throw aboard the LST was caught by the wind and whipped away. He recoiled the line and tried again, and then a third time, but it was evident from the start that his efforts were doomed to failure.

The tug bucked her way upwind and again the line flew out, but the wind caught it and while the lead thudded against the side of the LST, it struck just above the water line, many feet below the deck where the crew of the luckless vessel crouched.

A dozen times the tug strove to get a line aboard the drifting ship, but it was quickly evident that the effort was a wasted one. Nor could she get close enough to the LST to have any chance of getting a line about the end of the towing hawser. Any such attempt would have brought the two vessels crashing and grinding together and one or both might have had a side stove in.

The *Lucy Arkwright* did her best to help the stranded men, but there was nothing she could do that offered the slightest chance of success or of rescue. Both craft were drifting rapidly toward the shore and already the pounding of the surf could be plainly heard above the howl of the wind. At last the tug sheered off and lay to. A moment later a red rocket, followed by a second, streamed up into the air.

"Rockets!" Furness exclaimed. "We've got some too, in the ammunition locker. I'd like to trade them for a working radio, but they're better than nothing. Some one may see them."

With two members of the crew following, he fought his way across the deck and below. They returned with a box and a moment later a rocket streamed skyward from the LST. A second followed and then a third. Furness laid a restraining hand on the shoulder of the seaman who was firing them.

"Lay off," he said. "We've got only a dozen, so send them up at one minute intervals 'til you have four left, then at three minute intervals."

Sixty seconds later a fourth rocket soared upward from the doomed ship's deck. As it burst overhead there was a hoarse shout from one of the crew, a shout that was reechoed by the rest as they gazed shoreward. Three or four miles away, far beyond the line of pounding surf, a red light was blooming high in the air. Their signals of distress had been seen and answered.

"Life preservers!" Furness bawled. "Put on life preservers, all hands."

He tore one from the rack overhead and set the example by struggling into it and fastening the straps securely.

"A surfboat will probably come out," he shouted into the ears of his crew. "If it does, we'll have to jump over and they'll pick us up out of the water."

He looked at the tossing waves.

"Although how in the name of everything holy any crew can launch a surfboat or anything else in that water is beyond me," he muttered to himself.

"Distress Rockets at Sea, Sir!"

BILL DARROW SAT in the watch tower, huddled up in his pea jacket. The stove was going full blast but the heat it gave off was quickly dissipated by the howling wind which sought out every tiny crack and crevice in the many-windowed tower and poured into the room. The temperature in the room, he thought, must be down to freezing, possibly even lower, although the spray which beat constantly against the glass did not freeze. The inside of the windows was fogged and, despite his almost constant wiping of them, he could see out for only an instant at a time.

"What a night!" he grumbled as he rose and punched his watchman's clock. He pulled on his oilskins over the pea jacket, then cautiously opened the door to the platform. The wind caught it and almost tore it from his grasp. He leaned hard against it and shut it behind him, then edged around the corner of the tower where he felt the full force of the hurricane. For a moment he could hardly breathe, but he turned his head aside and, hanging onto the breast-high railing which edged the platform he worked his way around until he stood at the southeast corner.

He shielded his eyes as best he could with his hand and stared out to sea. He had not brought the binoculars with him for the spray would have rendered them worse than useless. Back and forth, from north to south, his gaze swept, but his eyes could see nothing but darkness and driving spray. The droplets of water stung like shot as they struck his exposed skin and the wind carried the water with such force that it sought out every seam and crevice in his oilskins and forced its way inside his protective covering. In a minute he was almost as cold and wet as though he had left his oilskins inside.

He gave one last look around, then turned back to the wind and started back for the shelter and comparative comfort of the tower. As he rounded the corner he gave, from force of habit, one last glance back at the sea. He stared unbelievingly, then rubbed his eyes to clear them of driven spray

"Distress Rockets at Sea, Sir!"

and looked again. He had made no mistake. Far out to sea a line of light had risen toward the sky to terminate in a flash from which a galaxy of stars had spun away to glow momentarily in the dark before they faded.

"Rockets!" he gasped. "Distress rockets!"

A second rocket arched its way skyward and Darrow was galvanized into action. He dashed around to the lee side and wrenched open the door of the tower. Not stopping to fight it closed, he snatched the telephone receiver and pressed the ring switch. There was no answering buzz in his ear and he realized that the instrument was dead. The falling flagpole had struck down the line and grounded the entire system.

Darrow did not hesitate. Tearing off the encumbering oilskins, he lifted the trapdoor in the tower floor. The wind poured in through the opening, but he caught a firm grip on the hand rail and started down the steps. The wind tore at him and strove to pluck him loose, but he hung on and made his way steadily downward. Once on the ground, the wind caught him and hurried him toward the station. It swept him past the door and almost slammed him into the corner of the building, but he checked his pace in time and fumbled with the door. The wind burst it open when he unfastened the catch and it took his full weight against it to close it once more. He hurried to Becker's room and hammered on the door.

The door opened almost instantly and Becker's huge bulk appeared. The Chief was fully clothed.

"What's the matter, Bill?"

"Distress rockets at sea, sir!"

"Where away?"

"Nor'east by north. About three miles out."

With an agility surprising in one of his weight, Becker jumped to the button of the alarm. The strident clanging of the gong rang through the station reinforced by Becker's stentorian shout.

"ALL HANDS! TURN TO!"

Even over the howling of the wind the thudding of feet could be heard as the crew tumbled out of their bunks and hurried, half clothed, to the locker room.

"Tell them oilskins and hip boots," Becker barked at Darrow. "I'm going up to take a look."

He fought his way up the tower and stared in the direction Darrow had given him. For thirty seconds only a Stygian darkness showed, then from the surface of the sea a streak of light winged its way skyward. Becker studied it, his mind making lightning calculations.

"Nothing between us for her to hang up on," he said. "She may founder, but if she don't, she'll pile up on the bar or on the beach, depending on her draft. She'll hit right close to the old light. It's a beach apparatus job, thank God, because this crew couldn't launch a boat in that surf."

He made his way inside the tower and took a Coston light from the locker. Back on the platform he fixed the holder in a socket and fired the light. An eerie red glow lighted up the tower, a signal to the distressed ship that her signals had been seen and that help was on the way. Satisfied that the light had been observed, Becker made his way down as rapidly as his bulk would permit. The crew were already gathered in the locker room when he arrived, Surfman with them.

"Go back in the tower, Bill," he said to Darrow. "Is the telephone working?"

"No, sir, it's dead."

"Radio?"

"I haven't tried it, sir, but it should be all right."

"If you can raise Oregon Inlet, tell Mr. Hargrove what's happened and that we're going out with the beach apparatus."

"Yes, sir."

"Then try to raise Chief Scarsdale at Little Kinnakeet and ask him to come on the run with every man he can muster. If we should have to launch a surfboat, it'll take both crews."

"Yes, sir."

"Turn to. Curly, get out the tractor and hook up to the beach cart. Take it to the old lighthouse, I think she'll come ashore or ground on the bar close to there. Jake, get out the command car. Barron, load in litters, blankets, ring life preservers and a couple of coils of one-inch line."

The crew scattered to their missions while Becker donned his oilskins, hip boots and a sou'wester. By the time the command car was loaded he was ready and he hoisted his bulk into the front beside Holman. A hundred yards ahead on the sandy trail the tractor was coughing its way forward, the beach apparatus cart with its Lyle gun and equipment bumping along behind.

At a warning blast from the command car's horn, Curly turned the tractor off the trail and allowed the faster vehicle to pass him, then swung back into the sandy ruts and went steadily ahead. As the command car turned from the trail toward the old lighthouse, two figures loomed up in its headlights. Head down, they were boring their way into the wind as best they could, but their progress was so slow as to be almost imperceptible.

"Jeff Davis and Old Joey," Becker exclaimed. "They'll never make it without a lift."

He laid a warning hand on Holman's arm and the command car slid to a stop. The two men crowded aboard and the car, its windshield wipers going

"Distress Rockets at Sea, Sir!"

steadily and ineffectually, bumped its way toward the old lighthouse tower which had stood, erect and steady, defying the storms of eighty winters. Holman drove past the tower and, using his four wheel drive, forced the command car up the revetment in front of the tower until the nose of his vehicle pointed straight out to sea on the top of the ridge, below which should lie the beach.

The beach was gone. Where, at low tide, a strip of sand should stretch for fifty yards to the edge of the surf, was now a boiling, seething mass of turbulent water. Twenty foot waves were pouring shoreward, driven by the force of the wind, to break against the ridge and hurl blinding clouds of spray high into the air. At a word from Becker, the crew and the two passengers dismounted, but as the wind caught them they were forced back until they stood huddled in a group below the ridge where they were partially sheltered from the roaring gale. Only Becker and Holman remained in the car.

"There she is!" Holman cried.

Half a mile offshore to the northeast, a rocket winged its way skyward. Becker nodded in satisfaction. His calculations had been correct. The ship would come ashore not over a hundred yards from the old lighthouse. He groped in the back of the car until he found a Coston light holder and a signal flare. A moment later the waves were illuminated by a red glare. Holman switched on the searchlight of the command car, but the powerful beam could not penetrate far enough through the spray-laden darkness to reveal the doomed vessel.

"Be ten minutes before she hits, maybe fifteen," Becker rumbled. "By that time we'll be ready for her. Curly should be here in another five minutes."

Aboard the drifting LST, Captain Furness and his crew felt a sudden lightening of their spirits as the red light gleamed so close to them. The *Lucy Arkwright*, which had followed them closely for several miles, had sheered away as the water began to shallow with their approach to the inner shoal. There was nothing more the tug could do to aid her lost tow and any closer approach to the shore might put two vessels in distress rather than one. The crew of the LST had realized this, but a feeling of terror and of abandonment overwhelmed them as their last forlorn hope pulled away and the lights of the tug bore away out to sea. The surf was coming perilously close and momentarily they expected to feel the grating, bumping sound on their keel which would mean that they had grounded and that the waves would pound with renewed vigor against the ship's side. Now they knew that brave men, men skilled in rescue work, were on shore waiting to aid them.

The LST drifted on. As she crossed the bar she

grounded with a sickening thud and heeled far over as the waves dashed against her side. Then she lifted, went ahead for a few yards, only to ground again. Only the bow was on the sand and the vessel swung around until she was headed directly into the wind, broadside to shore. Back and forth she whipped. Then the bow broke loose and the ship turned completely around, exposing her port side to the hurricane's force. Another surge of the water and she was over the bar into the channel between it and the beach.

She was past the outer line of surf, but the waves tossed her even more than before and the wind drove her steadily shoreward. In she came over the shelving beach until her bow ground into the sand. Once more the wind swung the stern until it appeared that she would end-around-end southward along the beach. But the stern struck and the ship heeled over to a forty degree list as the waves pounded against her exposed side. Captain Furness and his crew gathered in a bunch on the stern, hanging to the rail and straining their eyes toward the spot, two hundred yards away where the steady glow of the command car's headlights and searchlight boring into the spray and mist told of the presence of a rescue crew.

On the shore, Becker and his crew had watched the ship strike, but there was nothing they could do for the moment except to move the command car to a position directly opposite the LST where its lights faintly outlined the presence of the dark bulk. They were drenched with the driving spray and the force of the wind was so strong that they could stand only by leaning into the wind. A quarter of a mile back up the road the headlights of the tractor showed that it was crawling steadily forward, bringing with it the apparatus which might make the rescue of the crew of the stranded vessel possible. Becker took his place to windward of the crew, hoping that his commands would be audible.

"*Man the beach cart!*" he roared as Curly drove up.

His command was unintelligible, but the well-trained crew needed no orders to tell them what to do next. Quickly they loosed the cart from the tractor and took their places, then rolled the cart to the spot which Becker had already picked out. It was just below the ridge, partially sheltered from the force of the wind, for the beach where it would normally be located for such a rescue attempt was covered with boiling, churning water.

They spotted the cart, then took their places in formation, waiting for the Chief's next command.

Rescue

"ACTION!"

At Becker's command the crew burst into activity. Holman helped the Chief unload the Lyle gun and set it up on the windward side of the cart while Curly and Migert dragged the sand anchor to leeward and, with pick and shovel, began to dig a cross trench in which to bury it deep in the sand. A spare shovel lay beside the cart and Joey picked it up and took his place beside Migert while Curly swung industriously with the pick. Gradually the trench was deepened, although the diggers had to work stooped over and when they essayed to toss away a shovel of sand, the wind would catch the shovel blade and almost tear the tool from their grasp. Surfman dug industriously until Curly was forced to grab him by his collar and toss him to one side, out of the way.

"Think that'll do, Curly?" Migert bellowed in his companion's ear.

Curly shook his head and drove the pick again

into the packed sand, loosening it enough so that Migert and Joey could shovel it out. Becker, the gun emplaced, came up and looked into the trench with his flashlight.

"Bury it," he shouted in Curly's ear.

Curly hesitated a moment, then nodded in agreement and with the help of the others lowered the crossed timbers of the anchor into the trench. The shovels swung again as loose sand was filled into the trench, Curly tamping it down by treading back and forth across it. Surfman, despite his master's former rebuke of his activities, jumped into the trench beside Curly and helped to the best of his ability.

On the windward side of the cart Becker was prone, adjusting the Lyle gun. It had been set up on top of the ridge and Becker swung it into the wind, calculating as closely as he could the distance down wind the shot would be carried during its travel over the boiling water. Satisfied at last, he elevated the gun enough to ensure that the shot would carry the required distance, then rose to his feet.

Scarsdale and Ballard had brought the shot line box from the cart and placed it bottom up, three feet to windward of the gun, withdrawing the bottom board and faking pins. The long shot line, which had been carefully and evenly faked over the bottom board pins, lay in smooth coils in the box, ready to pay out evenly when the shot was fired.

Rescue

With a nod to Holman, Becker dropped the sack of powder down the bore of the gun. Holman came from the cart with the projectile in his hands. Scarsdale bent the end of the shot line to the projectile and Holman seated it in the barrel of the gun, pressing it down firmly on the charge. Becker loaded and inserted the firing mechanism, then stepped back, the firing lanyard in his hand.

He steadied the gun for a moment, then looked out to sea. The bulk of the stranded vessel could be dimly seen in the glare of the command car's lights. The light was dim, but there was no more to be had. The tractor was below the ridge, but Becker knew that its dim headlights would add little or nothing to the illumination.

"STAND CLEAR!" he roared.

The wind tore the words from his lips and carried them away, but a glance around showed him that the crew were standing behind the gun and well to one side. He bowed his head a moment in silent prayer, then jerked the lanyard.

The Lyle gun barked and leaped backwards. An orange flash split the darkness and the heavy projectile flew seaward, the shot line whipping out of the box and trailing after it. The flight of the projectile could be followed in the gleam of the lights and a groan came from Becker's lips. He had not made sufficient allowance for the force of the wind.

The shot disappeared into the darkness, but it was painfully evident that it had carried to the south of the LST and that the line would fall into the ocean and not across the stranded vessel.

The crew had watched the flight of the shot as eagerly as had Becker and they needed no fresh command. Scarsdale and Ballard tossed the nearly empty shot line box to one side and hurried back to the cart. In a few moments they were back with another box in which a spare line had been faked in preparation for just such an emergency.

Becker and Holman reemplaced the gun and Becker set it with meticulous care. Profiting by the experience of the first shot, he swung the muzzle more into the wind and slightly increased the elevation of the gun. The second shot line was heavier than the one used on the first shot and he knew that the wind would exert a stronger drag on it, not only carrying the projectile down wind, but also slowing its flight and shortening the range unless it were fired at a greater elevation.

Once more the gun was loaded and the crew stood back. There was a flash and a roar and the second projectile was on its way. Anxious eyes followed its flight and there was a cheer as the shot passed directly over the LST and the shot line fell across the deck of the stranded vessel. Communication with the men on the wreck had been established.

Rescue

Holman cut the shot line, leaving the unused portion in the box, and fastened the end to the tail block through which the whip lines, the lines which would pull the breeches buoy out to the wreck and back to the shore, were passed. Becker mounted the ridge and stood outlined in the glare of the command car's headlights. Leaning hard into the wind, he waved his arm in signal to the wreck. Standing beside him, Curly used a flashlight to blink a message out to sea. "Haul out," he flashed in the international code. "Haul out. Haul out."

Suddenly the shot line tightened. The men on the wreck had found it and, following instructions from the shore, were hauling it out to the vessel, and with it the tail block and the whip line. The tail block bumped across the ground and was lifted over the ridge by eager hands. It splashed down into the water but the men on the wreck were pulling steadily for yard by yard the whip lines, pulled off the reels by the crew members, moved out to sea. Presently the lines ceased moving and they knew that the block had been hauled on board. A bight of the lea whip was bent to the end of the hawser and the crew stood motionless, waiting for a signal from the wreck. It came at last in the form of the blinking of a flashlight through the storm, spelling out the letters "O.K." As the signal came, a car drove up and four volunteers from Buxton, who had seen the rockets and the glare of the Coston lights, came swarming up the bank, ready to aid where they were needed.

"MAN WEATHER WHIP!" was Becker's next command. "HAUL OUT HAWSER!"

Two members of the crew, aided by MacAlpin and the volunteers from Buxton, grasped the weather whip and hauled steadily on it while others tended the lea whip to prevent it from tangling with the hawser which Becker and Holman were hauling from the cart and lighting to the surf. When a flashed signal from the wreck told them that the end of the hawser had been secured on board, the breeches buoy was put on the hawser and secured with a clove hitch to the weather whip.

The shore end of the hawser was made fast to the sand anchor and all hands hauled it taut with a block and tackle. As the hawser lifted from the water, the wind caught it and pulled on it with terrific force. Under his feet Curly could feel the buried anchor give slightly and he shook his head doubtfully.

"I hope it holds," he muttered, then caught Joey by the arm and pulled him forward until the two men were standing directly over the anchor. Despite the hauling taut of the hawser, its weight still left it partly in the water, but once the crotch was raised, it would swing free above the surface.

On the top of the ridge, Becker and three other

men were struggling with the crotch. They got it under the hawser, but the task of raising it against the force of the wind proved to be almost more than they could accomplish. Joey and Scarsdale ran to help them and slowly the crotch rose. As the hawser was lifted out of the water, the pull of the wind increased and again the sand anchor moved uneasily under Curly's feet. The crotch was almost upright and the last few yards of the hawser came out of the water.

The wind tore at it and suddenly the hawser went loose as the sand anchor was ripped from the ground and flew seaward with the force of a cannon ball. The end of one of the heavy cross timbers struck Joey and tossed him a dozen feet away where he lay unconscious, blood oozing from a six inch gash in his scalp.

Curly, who had been standing over the anchor, was tossed aside, but he scrambled to his feet unhurt and ran to the aid of the crew. He tripped and the force of the wind caught him. He struggled to hold his footing, but the wind was too strong and he fell headlong, hitting Becker who was struggling to his feet, and dashing him again to the ground.

Becker heaved himself up to his knees. For once in his life his deep religious convictions and his early training were forgotten. A lurid stream of the purest and more forceful seagoing profanity came boiling from his lips. He grabbed Curly and bellowed in his ear.

"Get that —— —— of a —— tractor," he roared, "and bend that —— hawser to it. Then drive the —— —— thing out of here and haul that —— hawser taut. No —— —— sand anchor will hold in such a —— gale as this —— —— one is."

Curly gave a start and then shook with laughter as he crawled back behind the ridge, then got to his feet and ran to the tractor. The Chief might content himself with mild language and frown heavily on any expression stronger than "doggoned," but he was human after all.

Curly started the tractor and backed it up toward the cart. Willing hands fastened the hawser end to the tractor drawbar and Curly backed up. The sand anchor came slowly back over the ridge. The crotch was again put in place and the drag of the tractor slowly raised it to an upright position. Becker's arm shot upright and Curly stopped the tractor and set his brakes firmly before he ran once more up the slope to help in the rescue.

"MAN LEA WHIP!" Becker shouted.

Willing hands grasped the line and pulled and the breeches buoy ran along the hawser out to the waiting men. A flashed signal from the wreck told them that the first man was in the buoy and the weather whip was manned. For a time it came in freely and easily as the breeches buoy with its burden ran down the sloping hawser, but when the buoy reached the low point, the line came taut. The crew hauled it steadily in. There was a cheer as Becker and Holman lifted a drenched and half-frozen man from the breeches buoy and wrapped him in a blanket.

"How many on board?" Becker bawled into the rescued man's ear. The seaman's teeth were chattering so much that he could not manage coherent speech, but he spread his fingers wide.

"Five?" Becker asked and he nodded in assent.

Three more times the breeches buoy was hauled out to the stranded LST and each time a numbed and exhausted man was taken from it. Twice, as the pounding waves drove the LST higher on the beach, Curly started the tractor and took up the slack in the hawser, striving to keep it high enough above the surface of the water that the rescued men would not be entirely submerged during their perilous trip along the hawser to the shore.

The buoy was hauled out for the last time. Again came a flash from the wreck and the weather whip was manned. The line came in easily for a time, then came taut. Suddenly the line held firm. The men manning it started to haul in but a stentorian shout from Becker stopped them. The spray had momentarily died down and the length of the hawser was visible almost to the wreck. The breeches buoy was only a hundred yards away and there was a man in it, but the reason for the resistance of the line was evident. As the buoy had approached the surface of the water, the man in it had become panic stricken. He had risen in the buoy and had grasped the hawser with both hands, clinging to it with a death grip. He had striven to lift himself above the surface of the water and in doing so, had pulled himself almost out of the buoy. Had his feet not become entangled in the holes through which his legs had been thrust, the buoy would have been hauled in to shore empty, leaving the man dangling from the hawser until his strength failed and the pounding waves dragged him away to death.

The weather whip was quickly manned and the buoy pulled back until it was against him, but his legs were in the water and the buoy could not be pulled under him. Nor would it have availed had it been, for all sense had left the man and he clung to the hawser desperately with failing strength. It was a matter of minutes, possibly even of seconds, before his strength would fail and his grip slacken.

Becker cupped his hands and bellowed at the top of his lungs, but the wind caught his words and tossed them away, Even had they carried, they would have been useless, for the man's failing consciousness would not have comprehended their meaning, nor would his set muscles have obeyed their orders. No boat was at the beach, nor could one have been launched and live in the surf. It was impossible to haul in the empty buoy and send a man out in it, for the man's legs were tangled in the breeches and a pull on the whip would simply have dragged him from his hold on the hawser.

Even though he realized the futility of such an action, Becker was about to send back for the surfboat, but as he turned to give the order, he gasped.

"No, Curly, you can't!" he shouted and ran toward the end of the hawser. "*Come back here, you fool!*"

Curly did not heed the command. He had seen the situation as clearly as had Becker and he knew that long before the command car could reach the station, let alone return to the beach towing the surfboat, the man's grip on the hawser would have failed and he would have been washed away. There was only one chance of saving him and Curly was afraid to calculate how slight that chance was.

He stripped off his oilskins, his hip boots and his sweater, then leaped upward and caught the hawser in front of the crotch with both hands. He hung on a moment to make certain that his grip was firm, then began to work his way, hand over hand, out along the hawser toward the dangling man. It was a mad adventure at best and his chances of success were too small to be worth reckoning. There was a splash in the surf as Surfman sprang in to follow his master.

"COME BACK HERE!" Becker roared, but Curly paid no heed to the Chief's orders. The slope of the rope was downward and, but for the drag of the gale and the steady drenching from the spray, the task would not have been a difficult one. Below him, Surfman was dashed against the ridge, but as the wave rolled back he was carried out and he swam with all of his strength. Gradually he won free of the turmoil at the edge of the surf and swam steadily seaward.

Foot by foot Curly made his way out. The breaking waves caught at his feet and legs and dragged at him, but he hung on with both hands until each crest passed, then once more stubbornly resumed his progress. Thirty yards he made, forty yards, and then fifty. Now his legs were in the water all of the time and progress became slower and more difficult. Sixty yards, seventy, and Curly paused for an instant of rest, but rest was impossible. The drag of the wind and water was almost as bad when he hung on as it was when he made his way along the rope. The only advantage was that he was beyond the point where the waves broke into surf, but their crests still exerted a relentless drag on him.

Eighty yards, ninety, and now the man was close at hand. Curly's strength was failing, but he summoned it for a last effort. Ninety-five, a hundred, and then his groping hand struck the block of the breeches buoy and he knew that he had won through.

He shook his head to free his eyes from spray. Below him the ring of the buoy rose and fell on the water. The breeches had been pulled inside out and the feet of the man he had come to help were tangled in them. Curly studied the situation, then released the grip of one hand on the hawser and caught the bridle of the buoy. An instant later he was in the water and was pulling the buoy under the dangling man. The waves tossed him like a cork, but he kept his grip with one hand while with the other he strove to get the breeches back inside the ring of the buoy. At last he succeeded but the man's hands were still locked on the hawser and any haul from the shore on the whip line would once more pull the buoy out from under him. If the man were to be hauled to shore, his grip on the hawser must be broken.

Curly shook his head again, then waited for the crest of a wave to lift him. As he was raised, he reached up and caught the hawser. The crest passed and the hawser lifted him nearly out of the water, but he hung on and dragged himself up until his fingers found and gripped the seaman's wrist. He wrenched at the wrist to no avail, then strove to pry the clutching fingers from the hawser. One by one he opened them, but each time the opened finger would close as he felt for the next one.

Curly's strength was ebbing fast. As a last effort, he gripped the man's wrists with both hands and waited. A wave lifted them until the hawser was almost at the water's surface. It passed and the buoy dangled clear. Curly threw his weight downward with a jerk. The man's hold on the hawser was broken and he dropped into the breeches buoy, but Curly was swept away before he had time to make a grab for the bridle.

The crew on shore had watched the valiant battle by the light of the command car's lights and they gave a cheer as Curly broke the seaman's grasp and brought him down into the buoy and safety, but the cheer changed to a groan as the Coastguardsman was swept away into the sea. Swiftly the breeches buoy was hauled to shore and the now unconscious seaman taken from it.

"HAUL OUT!" Becker roared and the empty buoy was hauled out to sea. Curly's head could no longer be seen but Becker knew that somewhere in that raging swelter of water, he was fighting for his life. Running out the buoy was the only thing they could do to help him. It was a faint chance at best, but at least, if Curly could win to a grip on it, it might offer him a haven of safety.

When his grip on the seaman's wrist was broken, Curly went down into the water, down, down, down for what seemed miles. Although he had removed his oilskins and boots before starting his mad trip out along the hawser, he was still fully clothed and his watersoaked clothing dragged him down.

Down he went until his lungs seemed about to burst from the pressure, but he held his breath and swam in what he hoped was an upward direction. Sparks flashed before his eyes and in his ears was a steady, dull roaring. His mouth seemed full of blood and he longed to open it, to let the clean seawater wash the sickening taste away. His senses reeled and suddenly he knew that he could do no more. The end had come. His mouth fell open and the water poured in. There was a burning pain as the salt water struck his throat and in a moment he was fighting again, fighting in desperate panic, fighting against a choking that sent stabs of pain through him and changed the sparks of light before his eyes into dancing whorls of color. Then suddenly his head was above water and he was drawing in great lungsful of life-giving air. What matter that it was so mixed with spray as to be almost strangling, it was life, life itself, and he sucked it in avidly.

Once more the water closed over him, but now

he was fighting, not wildly and aimlessly, but with a dogged purpose. He knew where the surface was and he swam toward it. Again his long-held breath seemed intolerable, but he would not give in. At last his head was above surface and he greedily filled his lungs.

This time he was not pulled under, for a vagary of the waves buoyed him up and kept him afloat. He shook his head and looked around as a wave lifted him on its crest. On the shore he could see the glare of lights and, better than that, the hawser dangled only a few feet away. If he could reach it, he would have a chance.

He was tired, desperately tired, but he swam doggedly toward it. The waves tossed him about but he persisted, shaking his head when he had a chance, and fighting his way forward—or was he going forward? Curly could not tell, for it seemed as though the hawser which offered at least a temporary haven of safety was gradually withdrawing farther from him. He was so tired that his efforts seemed pointless. His stroke was no longer sure and steady, but merely an aimless thrashing of the waves. There was no use in battling longer. He ceased his struggles and let himself go limp. Safety lay only a few yards away, but it was not worth the battle to reach it.

Something bumped against him and there was a

stab of pain in his numbed arm. Languidly he tried to move the arm, but it was held fast. Something was pulling on it. He heard a familiar sound over the howling of the wind and the splashing of the waves. For a moment he wondered dully what it could be. It came again and an electric shock seemed to run through him. It was a bark, a muffled bark, and it came from his arm. Suddenly consciousness of his predicament returned to Curly and he shook his head violently. Swimming powerfully through the turbulent water, his master's arm gripped firmly in his strong teeth, was the Chesapeake.

"Surfman!" Curly gasped.

There was no time to wonder about the matter. Another wave broke and buried both of them, but the dog's grip did not slacken, nor did Curly again despair. They were under water for only a brief moment and when his head came up, Curly saw that the hawser was nearer. Better than that, the breeches buoy was dangling from it, only a few yards away. He summoned his few fragments of remaining strength, kicked violently, and struck out with his free arm.

Surfman's powerful muscles stood them in good stead. Despite the wind and the mountainous waves, inch by inch they won their way forward. Half the time they were buried under masses of water and once they were tossed almost clear, but they fought on. Now the buoy was only a yard away, now only eighteen inches. Another huge wave buried them in its depths, but as they came to the surface, the buoy was at hand. A desperate reach and Curly's fingers closed around one of the bridle ropes. A moment later he was clinging to the buoy with both hands while Surfman bobbed in the sea beside him.

He rested for a minute, then strove to climb into the buoy, but he was more exhausted than he realized. He pulled, but his arm muscles would not respond with enough strength to lift him up. Another wave struck him and one hand was torn loose. He hung on doggedly until the wave crest passed, then once more strove to lift himself. From the tail of his eye he saw another huge wave approaching. This one would tear him loose, he knew. Desperation gave him strength he did not know was left in his exhausted muscles. With a final effort he swung himself up and got his leaden legs over the ring of the buoy.

The wave tossed him about but his grip held. As the trough came, his feet slipped through the holes in the breeches and he was safe. On shore another cheer rang out and the haul home was started. A muffled bark came from the sea and panic shot through Curly. Where was Surfman?

Like a flash his hands shot up and grabbed the

hawser. For a moment he was sure the buoy would be pulled out from under him, but the crew on shore had seen his movement and they ceased hauling. Curly tried to drag the buoy out to sea, but he was too weak to make progress. On shore, Becker was watching intently. He turned and gave a sharp command. The lea whip was manned and slowly, a foot at a time, the buoy with its occupant was hauled seaward. Curly released his grip on the hawser and sank down into the buoy, staring out at the seething waters.

Suddenly he gave a gasp of relief. Only a few yards away a red head showed momentarily on the surface. Surfman was still swimming and his strength, despite the battering he had received, was far from exhausted. Foot by foot the dog came nearer until Curly's outstretched hand gripped his collar. A quick lift and his paws hooked over the ring of the buoy. Curly pulled with what strength remained in his tired arms. A wave lifted them and in another moment the Chesapeake had clambered in and Curly was holding him close.

Becker gave a fresh command and the buoy with its double burden moved rapidly shoreward.

The world spun crazily around Curly. He tried to steady it, but the effort only made the whirling worse. There was a burst of multicolored flame and Curly felt himself falling, down—down—down—

"Your actions tonight, Morgan," Jeff Davis Mac-Alpin said three hours later as he sat beside Curly's bunk at the station, "arouse in me distinctly mixed emotions; a mixture of reverence, amazement and disgust. You performed the most outstanding feat of sheer heroism I have ever witnessed or heard creditably of. At the same time, you showed a total disregard of your duty to preserve the life with which the Almighty endowed you. And, to cap it all, it was absolutely the most damphool act I have ever seen."

"Well, ——it, why shouldn't I have done it?"

"Morgan, your language is reprehensible," Mac-Alpin exclaimed.

"I'm merely quoting the Chief," Curly said with a grin. "Didn't you hear him when that sand anchor tore loose?"

"That is one of tonight's incidents that I prefer to forget. As to your question, I presume there is no valid reason why you should not have done it, since you succeeded. Had you failed, I could find a thousand."

"Gee whiz, Mr. MacAlpin, it wasn't anything. Any of the boys would have done the same thing, if they'd thought of it."

"I doubt that, Morgan. I believe there were only two persons present tonight with little enough common sense and sanity to try such a stunt—you and Surfman. And, as far as Surfman goes, it's like master, like man. You can't expect him to show any markedly better judgment than does the person whom he unreasoningly accepts as the source of all wisdom. Surfman, do you agree with me?"

The big Chesapeake, none the worse for his pounding by the water, thumped the floor vigorously with his tail.

"How are the men we hauled off coming along?" Curly asked.

"All of them are now in the arms of Morpheus, aided no doubt by Merle's administrations from the medical chest. None of them are, I believe, any the worse for their brush with death. The only serious casualty of the evening is our mutual friend, Joey. He has a broken collar bone and three ribs smashed in. In addition, he has either a severe concussion or a fractured skull. Time will tell which."

"Where is he?"

"He is in Merle's bed and Merle is beside him. We are doing all we can for him in the absence of competent medical help. Our radio is working and Norfolk is aware of the situation, but they are as helpless as we are. As soon as the weather permits, a doctor will be sent here and, if he so recommends, Joey will be taken to the hospital."

"Gee, I hope he gets along all right."

"So do I, Morgan, for several reasons, not the least of which is that he is one of my few real friends. Since you do not need my healing administrations, I will repair to his bedside. Merle is listening to him, but since my memory is better and my knowledge of the world greater than his, it is better to have two listen to him than one."

"Listen to him? What do you mean?"

"He has been talking steadily for the past two hours, despite our best efforts to quiet him."

"What's he talking about?"

"That, Morgan, is something about which you need not concern yourself—for the present. Now, before I leave, I desire you to swallow this pill which Merle has given me from the medical chest. If the information on the bottle from which it was taken is correct, it will guarantee you several hours of refreshing, dreamless and sin-free sleep. No, Surfman, I have no pill for you. Neither do you need one. I have yet to see the time when you could not sleep upon the slightest excuse. Good night, Morgan, I will see you when you awake. Good night, Surfman, pleasant dreams."

The Chesapeake rose and paced beside MacAlpin as far as the door. There, with a wag of his tail, he turned back to his master's bedside. He licked

Curly's hand for a moment, then turned around three times and sunk to the floor. His head dropped on his paws and in another minute he was sound asleep. The labors of the night had taken a toll from his strength, great as it was.

A Matter of Justice

CAPTAIN AINSLEE STRAIGHTENED UP in his chair.

"Thank you, Mr. Hunter, I think that will be all, unless— Does any member of the board wish to question this witness further?"

"Yes, I do," Commander Robinette said. "Mr. Hunter, there is one thing about your testimony that is not clear to me. I don't see how, after so many years, you could locate this body, not being certain what you were seeking, yet as soon as you found it, you could positively identify it and tell the story of the burial in great detail. Can you explain that?"

Old Joey rubbed his chin and thought for a minute before answering.

"No, Commander, I can't. It's just as I told you. For over twenty years I could remember things that happened to me the day before, or the year before, but back of one specific date, I could remember nothing. I had dreams and at times it seemed to me that I was going to remember, but I never did. I didn't know who I was nor how I got here on the Outer Banks.

"Then came the night of the storm. I went down with Mr. MacAlpin to help on the rescue and, as the storm came up, things became clearer and I was sure I was going to remember. Then came a smash and the next thing I knew, I woke up in the Marine Hospital in Norfolk.

"When I woke, I could remember everything that happened twenty years ago in great detail, up to a certain point. I could remember the storm that wrecked my boat and the way a surfman came out and rescued me when I had given up all hope. He got me into the water, and there my memory stopped. After that, everything was a blank, except that I knew there was something hidden, something that I must dig up. I didn't remember what it was, but I could remember where it was.

"When I returned to Avon, I got help from the Coast Guard station and we started searching. We dug around for two days and were about to give up when Surfman, a dog belonging to Machinist's Mate Graham, one of the searchers, exhumed a bone. We dug where he had been digging and in a few minutes we had the entire skeleton uncovered. As soon as I saw it, the whole thing came back to me like a flash.

I remembered waking up on the beach and finding the man who had rescued me, lying dead beside me. I remembered burying him, then starting out to look for help, but there my remembrance ended and ends.

"I cannot remember anything from that moment until I woke in the Marine Hospital. I do not know or remember men whom I have known on the Outer Banks for years. Even Jeff Davis MacAlpin and Curly Graham, who were my closest friends, are now new acquaintances, although I can dimly feel that I have known them before, but it is an instinctive feeling, not a matter of knowledge. When I came back to Avon, I did not even know where my home was, nor did I recognize my own boat."

"It seems mighty queer to me—" Commander Robinette began, but Dr. Heinrichs, the Public Health Service officer who was consultant to the Coast Guard Investigating Board, interrupted.

"Commander, the matter may not be understandable, but it is wholly believable. We know little about the workings of the human mind, especially where amnesia is concerned. The severe blows which Mr. Hunter received, not only twenty years ago, but also two months ago, are unquestionably responsible for the vagaries of his memory. Cases similar to his are rare, but are of definite record."

"Well . . . No more questions, Captain."

A Matter of Justice

Captain Ainslee looked around the table.

"Any further questions? There appear to be none. The board will retire. Will all witnesses please remain available in case they are to be recalled?"

The members of the board rose and left the room. Mary Truslow put her handkerchief to her lips.

"What will they do now, Morgan?" she asked in a trembling voice.

Curly put his arm around her.

"Don't worry, Mother," he said. "Things are coming out all right. Dad's body was positively identified and Joey's story was clear."

"But will they clear his name?" she persisted.

"I can't see, Mrs. Truslow," Jeff Davis MacAlpin said, "that they have any choice in the matter. The evidence is clear and I think my supporting brief sums up all the loose ends."

"It was a wonderful brief, Mr. MacAlpin, and I don't know how I'll ever be able to repay you for all the days you spent on it, and all the trips you made to Washington about it, and everything else you did."

"All of that, my dear woman, sprang from crass selfishness. I am primarily a newspaperman and I saw a story, a darned good story and one that I can sell for a price, in the affair. I was prompted in my endeavors by purely mercenary considerations, not by those of justice or of altruism—"

"Jeff," Merle Becker broke in, "that's the first deliberate lie I've ever known you to tell."

MacAlpin had the grace to blush.

"Perhaps, after all, it is a matter of justice," he said. "Hello, here they come back. It didn't take them very long to reach a conclusion."

The members of the board were reentering the room. They took their seats at the table and Captain Ainslee cleared his throat.

"Mrs. Truslow, as the most interested party, I am going to address my remarks to you. This board has considered all of the evidence brought forth and has arrived at the following conclusions."

He consulted a paper in his hand and went on.

"Surfman Stanton Truslow did, on the night of March 16, 1929, while on beach patrol, see a fishing vessel wrecked on the inner shoals off the beach on the southern edge of Cape Hatteras. The emergency was too great to allow of a delay to summon assistance and he did, with extreme bravery and with commendable devotion to duty, at once undertake the task of rescue. At the risk and, as it turned out, at the cost, of his life, he did succeed in rescuing and saving the life of one Joseph Hunter, owner of the wrecked vessel.

"The board further finds that Mr. Hunter, while in a state of complete amnesia, did bury the body of Surfman Stanton Truslow and failed to inform any-

A Matter of Justice

one of his actions and that the body lay buried in an unknown spot until it was exhumed two weeks ago by Mr. Hunter, whose memory was partially restored by a severe blow on the head. The body exhumed has been positively identified.

"The board further finds that the name of Surfman Stanton Truslow was, on May 25, 1929, dropped from the rolls of the United States Coast Guard as having deserted the service in the face of danger, and that such action, in view of the evidence educed before this board, was in error. Do you understand this, Mrs. Truslow?"

"Ye—yes, sir."

"The board, all the members agreeing, makes the following recommendations. That the name of Surfman Stanton Truslow be restored to the rolls of the United States Coast Guard and that it then be dropped with the notation, 'killed in line of duty while engaged in saving life.' The board further recommends that Surfman Stanton Truslow be posthumously awarded the Gold Life-Saving Medal of the Treasury Department for extreme bravery and heroic devotion above and beyond the call of duty."

Mary Truslow gasped.

"Then—then—his name will be cleared?"

"There is not the slightest question about it, Mrs. Truslow. Your husband will, belatedly, get the credit and recognition of which he has, through circumstances beyond control of the Coast Guard, been unjustly deprived for twenty years. And I will make it my great pleasure, Mrs. Truslow, to personally assist you in obtaining the pension to which you are justly entitled.

"Before closing this case, the board wants to thank Mr. Joseph Hunter for his actions and testimony and to acknowledge and give thanks for the great and valued help given to the board by Mr. Jeff Davis MacAlpin.

"We have another matter for our attention before we adjourn. Machinist's Mate Morgan Graham."

"Yes, sir."

Curly sprang to his feet with a puzzled expression and faced the board.

"I have here an application from you for a change of name, supported by a certified copy of a decree from a court of competent jurisdiction. This application has been approved and your name has been changed on the rolls of the Coast Guard to Morgan Graham Truslow. I hand you a warrant for your rating, made out in your new name."

Curly took the paper with a swelling heart and looked proudly at it. Suddenly his face dropped and he handed the paper back.

"I'm sorry, Captain, sir," he said, "but this is wrong. It says Machinist's Mate, 1st Class, not 2nd Class."

A Matter of Justice 249

Captain Ainslee's face broke into a smile.

"That's no error, Truslow. And may I add that the recommendation for the Silver Life-Saving Medal to you for bravery has been modified to conform both to your new name and to your new rating."

"My—my medal—Gosh!"

Mary Truslow threw her arms about her son and tears rolled down her face. Captain Ainslee looked momentarily away.

"I think that concludes the business before the board," he said. "We stand—"

"Just a minute, Jimmy," Jeff Davis MacAlpin broke in. "It seems to me that this august body is leaving some unfinished business if it adjourns now."

"Why, no, I think— What the devil are you talking about, Jeff?"

"Well, you've satisfactorily taken care of several people, but you've completely neglected one of the most important. What are you going to do for Surfman? I've already recommended that he be made a Chief Bo'sun's Mate and given charge of a station."

Captain Ainslee laughed.

"I agree with you, Jeff, but about all we can do is to offer him our congratulations and to tell him that each of us wish we had a dog half as good. We can't award him a medal, much as we think he deserves one. I think his recognition is a matter which must be taken care of by his local station."

"We'll take care of it all right," Merle Becker rumbled. "We'll make him a medal, two or three of them if he wants them, and I'll award it to him at a full muster of the crew. How about it, Surfman, will you trust us to take care of it?"

The big Chesapeake, who was crowding close to his master and licking Mary Truslow's hand, wagged his tail enthusiastically.

Appendix

I

The United States Coast Guard

THE UNITED STATES COAST GUARD, although it has existed under its present name and in its present form only since January 28, 1915, lays claim with considerable justice and authority to the proud title of "The Oldest Seagoing Armed Force." The red and white barred Coast Guard ensign and pennant have flown unchanged since their adoption in 1799.

The Revenue Cutter Service, the immediate predecessor and one of the two organizations consolidated in 1915 to form the Coast Guard, dates from August 4, 1790, when the Congress passed an act to provide for a more effective method of collecting the customs. This act, which was passed on the urgent recommendation of Alexander Hamilton, the first Secretary of the Treasury, authorized the construction of ten "Revenue Cutters" to be used to prevent smuggling and to enforce the collection of the customs duties levied by the new republic.

This action was a necessity. During the colonial period, smuggling, which was evading the "taxation without representation" levied by the English Parliament on the North American colonies, was not only a laudable, but also a patriotic act. The best people of the colonies not only condoned, but actively aided the smugglers, and most of them were not averse to an actual participation in the illegal trade. However, when independence became a fact and not a political theory, smuggling took on a different aspect. It was no longer to be condoned, let alone praised, but old habits are hard to break and Alexander Hamilton found that thousands of dollars of potential revenue were daily escaping the federal treasury through the illicit entry of dutiable merchandise.

The new "Treasury fleet" as it was then called (and frequently still is) was duly put in commission and for nearly ten years was the only fleet which the United States had, for it was not until April 30, 1798 that the Navy Department came into being. Almost at once a number of the revenue cutters were placed under the orders of the newly created

Appendix: THE U. S. COAST GUARD 253

Navy Department and they took a very prominent part in the hostilities with France. This transfer was at first made solely by departmental action and without the authority of law, a situation which was remedied on February 25, 1799, by the passage of "An Act for the Augmentation of the Navy" by the Congress.

The close association between the Revenue Cutter Service and the Navy, which was started by Alexander Hamilton when he recommended that the officers of the treasury fleet be commissioned as officers of the navy (advice which the Congress saw fit to ignore) has persisted throughout our entire history. In every war that the United States has fought, the revenue cutters have borne their full share of the fighting and their record is a very enviable one.

The second organization which was consolidated with the Revenue Cutter Service to form the Coast Guard was the Lifesaving Service of the Treasury Department. Although lifesaving installations had been established on a voluntary basis for many years (The Massachusetts Humane Society, which built crude huts along the Massachusetts coast and offered rewards to anyone who made "signal exertions" in rescuing life from the sea, dates from 1785) it was not until 1847 that the first step was taken by the Congress to establish such activities on an official footing. The first steps were meager ones, but in 1854, the service was put on a slightly firmer basis by authorizing the employment (at $200 per year!) of "keepers" for the boat houses which had been built. However, things went from bad to worse. Capable, reliable men could not be obtained for $4.00 per week and most of the appointments degenerated into mere political plums.

In 1871 a change came. Sumner I. Kimball, newly appointed Chief of the Treasury Department's Revenue Marine Division, took hold of the boathouses with a firm hand. Development and improvement came rapidly and when the Congress, in 1878, set it up as a self-contained bureau with a General Superintendent, Kimball was obviously the man for the newly created position.

The history of the Lifesaving Service is filled with countless feats of outstanding heroism. Regardless of weather, the intrepid lifesavers went out, although, sad to say, many times they failed to come back. During its forty-four years of existence as an organization, they have a record of 177,286 lives saved.

Development under Kimball's rule was rapid. Stations were built along the coasts, beach patrols were established, new equipment—Lyle guns, Coston lights, surfboats, breeches buoys—was developed which added to the efficiency and usefulness

Appendix: THE U. S. COAST GUARD 255

of the Life Boat Stations. By 1915, the Lifesaving Service had grown to 280 stations along the Atlantic, Pacific and Gulf coasts, the Great Lakes and one station at the Falls of the Ohio River, near Louisville, Kentucky. The last big job of the Lifesaving Service as such was in 1913 when they raced overland to bring aid to the flood-stricken regions of Kentucky, Ohio, Indiana and Illinois.

With the improvement of equipment, particularly with the more rapid movement permitted along the coast line by the use of motor vehicles, the number of stations steadily decreased and the distance between them became greater. There are fewer stations today than there were in former years, but the existing stations are more efficient and are equipped to cover promptly a longer stretch of coast than were their predecessors. While the number of wrecks has decreased, due to the use of radio and the universal use of power instead of sails on seagoing vessels, the Life Boat Stations have far from outlived their usefulness. I found that the stations I visited had an average throughout the year of about one rescue call per week, abundant evidence to my mind that they are not "on their way out" as I have heard some persons state.

On January 28, 1915, the Revenue Cutter Service and the Lifesaving Service were combined to form the United States Coast Guard, but the organization was not yet complete. In 1939 the Lighthouse Service, originally established as a bureau of the Treasury Department, but since 1903 a bureau of the Department of Commerce and Labor, was consolidated with the Coast Guard and became an integral part of it. This gave the Coast Guard jurisdiction over the lighthouses and other navigational aids in United States waters.

During the years of its existence, the Revenue Cutter Service often had to function as a handy man for the other government departments and it picked up a number of unusual and little known duties, such as suppression of the slave trade, enforcement of the neutrality laws, suppression of piracy, suppression of smuggling, conservation of timber resources, rendering assistance to vessels in distress and the saving of life and property at sea. Most of these strangely assorted duties, which until quite recently still devolved upon the Coast Guard, meaningless as they were, have been eliminated by a new recodification of the law. This is an excellent thing, for the Coast Guard has a tremendous variety of duties on its hands without bothering about obsolete laws, interesting as they might have been, from a historical viewpoint.

Not only do the Coast Guard cutters go to the aid of vessels in distress, they also maintain the International Ice Patrol, the weather patrol, the Bering

Sea Patrol, the pelagic (fur seal) patrol, the Alaskan patrol and a number of others, while their ice breakers are constantly engaged in the strenuous work of keeping harbors open during the winter season. The Aids to Navigation section mans and maintains all lighthouses, as well as radio beacons, loran towers, daymarks, fog signals, and lighted and unlighted buoys variously equipped with whistles, bells, gongs and trumpets, to the number of over 30,000. The Life Boat Stations scattered along all of our coasts, including the Great Lakes, are constantly alert to save life and property and the Search and Rescue planes fly over a million miles a year on errands of mercy.

The Coast Guard of today is a uniformed, military organization. It has ranks and ratings, commissioned, warrant and enlisted, and a pay and subsistence scale identical with that of the United States Navy. The uniforms of the two services are the same except for the Treasury shield which is worn on the right sleeve above the cuff by enlisted men and on both sleeves by officers. During peace it is a part of and operates under the Treasury Department, but upon the declaration of war, it automatically becomes an integral part of the Navy for the duration of hostilities. This has been of incalculable value to the Navy, for during World War II, Coast Guard personnel not only trained both Army and Navy personnel in amphibious warfare, but also spearheaded many of the beach landings made, especially in the Pacific theater. The part the Coast Guard played in World War II can best be summed up by the remark made by Admiral Bill Halsey to a wounded Coast Guard whom he visited in a hospital at Wellington, New Zealand:

"I know what you fellows have done. The Coast Guard did a damn good job there!"

No account of the Coast Guard can be considered at all complete without some reference to the United States Coast Guard Academy at New London, Connecticut. This school which is on a par with the Military and Naval Academies at West Point and Annapolis, has the distinction of being the only one of the service academies to which *all* admissions are on a strictly competitive basis. No political or other appointment need be obtained. There is no state quota or other similar limitation. Any United States citizen between the ages of seventeen and twenty-two who is a high school graduate may make application to the Commandant for admission. If he can satisfy the high scholastic, physical, and character requirements of the Coast Guard and ranks high enough on the list of those examined (about one hundred and fifty are selected annually out of some two thousand taking the examination) he will be admitted as a swab. Following a

Appendix: THE U. S. COAST GUARD

successful completion of the strenuous four year course, he will emerge from the academy with an excellent education, a modest bank account and a commission as an Ensign in the United States Coast Guard, the admission key to a long and honorable career, both afloat and ashore.

For anyone wishing to learn more of the Coast Guard, particularly its history and development through the years since 1790, I can strongly recommend the complete and accurate, yet popular and highly readable book, *Always Ready* by Kensil Bell.

II

The Cape Hatteras Light

CAPE HATTERAS, NORTH CAROLINA, with the Diamond Shoals extending eight miles to seaward, constitutes one of the greatest hazards to shipping on any coast of the United States. It has been said that every war in which the United States has fought, except the Mexican War, has been won or lost off Cape Hatteras. Because of its location in reference to shipping lanes, this area was one of the great battlegrounds of submarine warfare during both World War I and World War II.

The first light tower off Cape Hatteras was built in 1798 at the urgent recommendation of Alexander Hamilton, the first Secretary of the Treasury. This tower, which was ninety feet high, stood until it was replaced by a taller one in 1854. This, in turn, was replaced by a new tower, which still stands, in 1870. This is the tallest lighthouse in the United States, standing one hundred and ninety-three feet high. It is built of brick on a granite base and painted with broad black and white spiral bands. It was

Appendix: THE CAPE HATTERAS LIGHT 261

equipped with a first order lens having twenty-four panels. This lens revolved slowly, giving a flash every six seconds. It was a beautiful sight from near the tower to see these twenty-four beams of clear light sweeping around the horizon and an even more beautiful sight to the mariner at sea who knew that the light gleamed for his protection.

It was soon evident that a light on the cape was not sufficient for the safety of vessels. A lightship was built and placed on Diamond Shoals in 1824. After a few months this vessel broke from her moorings and was driven far out to sea, but it rode out the storm and made the port of Norfolk safely. The lightship was repaired several times, but finally in 1827 it was driven ashore near Ocracoke Inlet and wrecked.

Many attempts were made after 1827 to make some provision other than a lightship for Diamond Shoals. The building of a lighthouse, bell buoys, whistle buoys and light buoys were tried, but none of them proved successful. On September 30, 1897, the newly built Lightship No. 69 displayed her lights on the Diamond Shoals station. Since that date a lightship has been continuously maintained at this position, except for brief intervals when they were carried away by storms, or removed from station due to this country being at war.

The lighthouse tower on Cape Hatteras was used

from its building in 1870 until 1935 when it was temporarily abandoned and the light moved to a new steel tower located some two miles inland. While the old tower had been placed at what was considered a safe location in 1870, the sea and wind began to erode away the beach and to encroach on the tower to such an extent that its undermining and collapse were deemed imminent.

The old tower was abandoned to the custody of the National Park Service and was established as a National Monument and remained as such until 1942. During this period a series of wooden revetments were erected in an attempt to check the inroads of the ocean. Sand piled up against these revetments and was anchored by the planting of sea oats and other long-rooted vegetation. The project was entirely successful and the sea reversed its action and the beach is now building up and out. There seems to be no reason why the beautiful old tower should not stand for another eighty years or longer.

In 1942 the Coast Guard, impelled by the necessities of war, resumed control of the old tower and used it as a lookout station until 1945, when it was again offered to the National Park Service. However, some damage had been done to the tower while it was used as a lookout station and the National Park Service refused to accept responsibility. As a result,

Appendix: THE CAPE HATTERAS LIGHT 263

the tower was an orphan for the next four years and was subjected to various sorts of vandalism until the Coast Guard resumed control in 1949.

Since the danger of undermining by the sea had passed, it was decided that the new steel tower should be abandoned and the light replaced in the old tower. The tower was repaired, repainted and put in first-class condition. A new Marine Aero beacon type light of 250,000 candle power showing a flashing white light at fifteen second intervals was built and installed. The old tower, with all its beauty and grandeur, went back into commission in the fall of 1949, after sixteen years of darkness.

III

The Phonetic Alphabet

THE PHONETIC ALPHABET (which uses a word in place of a letter) is used by the Coast Guard and other radio operators for greater clarity and accuracy in transmission. Where the letters, "*A*", "*J*", and "*K*" might easily be confused, the corresponding phonetic letters, "*Able*", "*Jig*", and "*King*" are readily distinguishable. This alphabet is used when giving the call letters of a station and also when it is necessary to spell out a name or other word.

The alphabet used by the Coast Guard is:

Able	*Jig*
Baker	*King*
Charlie	*Love*
Dog	*Mike*
Easy	*Nan*
Fox	*Oboe*
George	*Peter*
How	*Queen*
Item	*Roger*

Appendix: THE PHONETIC ALPHABET

Sugar	*William*
Tare	*Xray*
Uncle	*Yoke*
Victor	*Zebra*

The call letters of all Coast Guard radios are *Nan Mike* (NM). For each district, another letter is added. Thus the call letters of the Fifth Coast Guard District at Norfolk, Virginia, are *Nan Mike Nan* (NMN). For each land station within the district, a number is added to the district letters to make a station call. Thus *Nan Mike Nan Two Three* (NMN 23) would be the call signal for the 23rd station of the Fifth District of the U.S. Coast Guard.

Ships and planes, which are frequently transferred from one district to another, have their own permanently assigned call letters (usually a four letter group) which is not affected by a transfer from one district to another. Thus *Nan Mike Dog Sugar* (NMDS) might be the call letters for the lightship stationed on Diamond Shoals and *Nan Mike Zebra King* (NMZK) might be the call letters of a Search and Rescue airplane stationed at Elizabeth City.

Two special words or signals are commonly used. One, *Roger*, is official and means, "I have received your last transmission satisfactorily." The other, which is unofficial, but which is frequently used, is "*Wilco*", meaning "Will comply" or "Sure, I'll do that thing."

IV
Beaufort's Scale

The velocity or force of wind is nautically reported in "forces" according to Beaufort's Scale and not in miles per hour. The following table shows the equivalent of each Beaufort number in miles per hour, both statute (land) miles and nautical (sea) miles, together with the terms used by the United States Weather Bureau in making forecasts.

Beaufort number	Miles per hour (nautical)	Miles per hour (statute)	Term used in Weather Bureau forecast
0	Less than 1	Less than 1	
1	1–3	1–3	Light
2	4–6	4–7	Light
3	7–10	8–12	Gentle
4	11–16	13–18	Moderate
5	17–21	19–24	Fresh
6	22–27	25–31	Strong
7	28–33	32–38	Strong
8	34–40	39–46	Gale
9	41–47	47–54	Gale
10	48–55	55–63	Whole gale
11	56–65	64–75	Whole gale
12	Above 65	Above 75	Hurricane

Appendix: BEAUFORT'S SCALE

When a conversion table is not available, the force may be roughly translated into nautical miles per hour by means of the following mariner's "rule of thumb."

Forces 1-3 Square the force
Forces 4-8 Multiply the force by four
Forces 9-11 Multiply the force by five

All persons and events in this story are fictitious, and any resemblance to any actual persons is purely coincidental.

A Note on the Type
IN WHICH THIS BOOK IS SET

This book was set on the Linotype in Janson, a recutting made direct from the type cast from matrices (now in possession of the Stempel foundry, Frankfurt am Main) made by Anton Janson some time between 1660 and 1687.

Of Janson's origin nothing is known. He may have been a relative of Justus Janson, a printer of Danish birth who practised in Leipzig from 1614 to 1635. Some time between 1657 and 1668 Anton Janson, a punch-cutter and typefounder, bought from the Leipzig printer Johann Erich Hahn the type-foundry which had formerly been a part of the printing house of M. Friedrich Lankisch. Janson's types were first shown in a specimen sheet issued at Leipzig about 1675. Janson's successor, and perhaps his son-in-law, Johann Karl Edling, issued a specimen sheet of Janson types in 1689. His heirs sold the Janson matrices in Holland to Wolffgang Dietrich Erhardt, of Leipzig.

COMPOSED, PRINTED, AND BOUND BY
H. Wolff, NEW YORK, N. Y.

CPSIA information can be obtained at www.ICGtesting.com
Printed in the USA
LVOW01s1053110114

368941LV00003B/623/P